Jumbo Shrimp
guide to

Italian
WINE

POSITIVE PRESS

author HOUSE

AuthorHouse™
1663 Liberty Drive
Bloomington, IN 47403
www.authorhouse.com
Phone: 833-262-8899

Published by AuthorHouse 03/18/2021

ISBN: 978-1-6655-1918-2 (sc)
ISBN: 978-1-6655-1919-9 (hc)
ISBN: 978-1-6655-1917-5 (e)

Library of Congress Control Number: 2021904624

Print information available on the last page.

Authors
Lyka Caparas, Jacopo Fanciulli,
Rebecca Lawrence, Lan Liu

Preface
Stevie Kim

Illustrations
Silvia Albano

CONTENTS

BIG THINGS COME IN SMALL PACKAGES
WELCOME TO THE JUMBO SHRIMP GUIDE

 Welcome to the Jumbo Shrimp Guide to Italian Wine. This guide is an *instant* book, and hopefully one of many in an ongoing series. The idea is not original; a quick introduction to the complicated and yet fascinating topic of Italian wine. We are lucky to have four dedicated and enthusiastic writers on board and whilst each one of them was vigorously opposed to the "Jumbo Shrimp" oxymoron title of the series, they lost - there is no democracy in the world nowadays!

In all seriousness, the Four Musketeers (Rebecca, Jacopo, Lyka and Lan) have managed to make a seemingly dense and unapproachable subject one that can be enjoyed with humour and lightness, without taking away from the intricacies that make it great. The thing that unites the book is that it is Italian wine seen through the eyes of people who love it, who are immersed in it, but who aren't necessarily Italian (okay, okay we threw in a Ligurian to keep us in check!). The aim is a simple guide to Italian wine, useful information, but also fun facts and some frivolities. It should educate but also amuse.

How to read this book and how much time is needed? Whilst our initial inspiration for a short book came from

Jancis Robinson's *The 24-hr Wine Expert*, (grazie mille Ms. Robinson!), our objective was not so much that you should become an Italian Wine Expert simply by reading this book (there are other more painful ways of becoming an Italian Wine expert, for that go to the back of the book for more info on the Vinitaly International Academy), but to begin the Italian wine conversation. You can read the entire book once, not necessarily in order, but more importantly you can go back to find some anecdotes and fun facts to impress your fellow wine lovers! We hope that some parts of this Jumbo Shrimp Guide will navigate you on your way to exploring more about Italian wine, and have you looking forward to the next book in the series. What's more, we've transformed parts of the book into an audio series for the Italian Wine Podcast, so now you can literally take your Jumbo Shrimp Guide wherever you go using your favourite podcast platform.

This book was a labor of love. Even for a small book like this, there was an incredible amount of coordination, generosity and time dedicated by every member of the team. In addition to the authors, I'd like to thank the talented Silvia with her fun drawings and Andrea who manned the entire project patiently but rigorously, respecting the timeline.

We love Italian wine, we hope you will too, even more after this book!

Stevie Kim

Party with Bacchus, dance with Italian wine

Bacchus (*Bacco* in Italian), the son of Zeus, was the Roman god of the grape harvest, winemaking, wine, and ecstasy. Much like his Greek equivalent Dionysus, Bacchus earned the title of party god. Throughout the central and southern Italian peninsula, the bacchanalia, a festival of Bacchus involving ecstatic elements, was very popular from 200 B.C. onwards. Though Bacchus was portrayed diversely by artists: some depicted him as a young, fit and long-haired man while others illustrated him as an older and bearded God, his passion and love for wine and parties were unquestionable. Legend has it that Bacchus spent his childhood with Silenus, a great wine lover, withwhom he completed his wine training. Then Bacchus travelled through Asia Minor, the Middle East, and the Mediterranean to transmit his knowledge of vine growing and winemaking to humans. Among the 12 Olympian Gods, Bacchus might not be the most powerful, but he was a favoured contender as the most popular, being the god of celebration and wine.

1. A BRIEF HISTORY OF ITALIAN WINE

Ancient Times to Renaissance

Wine in Italy has a long and distinguished history. It first became important in Southern Italy around 2000 B.C. thanks to Phoenician traders, and later around 1000 B.C. thanks to Greek colonists. These traders and colonists not only imported the vines planted in their own lands, but also new grapevine cultivation and vinification techniques. From Sicily, Puglia, and Calabria, they gradually spread northward. The Etruscans further boosted the spread of viticulture and winemaking, and were known for trellising their vines low and for pruning them regularly. Then of course, along came the ancient Romans and integrated the existing systems of viticulture into their own daily activities. They were well known for taking objects and practices from various people they came into contact with, not least because they often married into the families of people they conquered. It was the Romans that first referred to Italy as "Enotria," or the "land of wine". The etymology of this name comes from the habit of training vines on poles or posts as is normal today, instead of relying on trees or other plants. It was apparent to the ancient Romans that vines trained to poles gave better wines, and the importance of making good wine was not lost on the Romans! Ancient documents show that land holdings with vineyards trained to poles were sold for four times more than those in which vines were allowed to run wild.

Pliny the Elder

This ancient Roman (AD 23-79) had many professions. He was a philosopher, statesman and a military commander, but it's his writings about wine which have made him most famous. Known as one of the original wine critics, Pliny also gave us what is considered the  first-ever wine classification based on quality, roughly eighteen centuries before the 1855 classification in Bordeaux. In it he covered the best vineyard sites of regions stretching from Lombardy to Sicily, indicating which wines were the most sought after and why, how long they could age, when they were best drunk up, and which were the most expensive. Not surprisingly, Pliny dedicated 2 of 37 volumes in his lifetime masterpiece, *Encyclopedia Naturalis Historia* (Natural History), to wine. Volume 14 included a ranking of Rome's top vineyards, and volume 17 expounded upon the notion of terroir. Pliny wrote extensively about wines produced from Pompei where his life ended in the eruption of the Vesuvius volcano.

Owing to the many great intellectuals of the Roman era, for example Virgil, Horace, Ovid, Catullus, Juvenal and many others, we have come to know the extent of Roman viticulture, indeed. Before the 1855 classification in Bordeaux existed, it was Pliny the Elder who created what is thought to be the first ever wine classification system based on quality.

With the Barbarian invasions and the fall of the Roman Empire, Italy's viticulture went into rapid decline, but grapevines and winemaking survived, essentially, thanks to the Church (clearly, wine was needed for Sunday Mass). Viticulture and winemaking were to flourish in Italy again only many years later, in the Feudal age, when the economic wealth that wine production could bring was evident and strict laws were implemented in order to protect vines.

It was in the Middle Ages that many innovations in wine production came into effect, including many that seem so obvious to us now:

- The separate vinification of white and red grapes (rather than just pressing them altogether);
- Variability in the length of maceration on the skins;
- The first accurate zonation attempts of vineyards, for example recognising that wines made from grapes grown on better exposed sites (such as the top of the hill) fetched higher prices;
- The introduction of legislation designed to define the timing of the harvest and to regulate the production and trade of wine.

Eighteenth and Nineteenth Centuries

The nineteenth century was decisive for oenology thanks to great scientific progress, leading to a better understanding of grape varieties and winemaking. For example, it was Louis Pasteur's mid-nineteenth-century discovery of the role played by yeasts in alcoholic fermentation that allowed winemaking to propel itself into the modern era. It is also in the second half of the nineteenth century that many of Italy's most famous wines became established, such as Brunello di Montalcino and modern day Chianti in Tuscany.

Phylloxera and World Wars

At the end of the nineteenth and the beginning of the twentieth century, parasites and fungi devastated Europe's vineyards. The first was Oidium (or powdery mildew) that attacked grapevines in Liguria and Piedmont, destroying much of the vineyards, soon followed by Peronospora (or downy mildew). In 1879, phylloxera, the worst of all the grapevine pests, appeared in Italy, at first mainly in Lombardy and Sicily, but from these two places it slowly spread throughout the rest of the country. An aphid that feeds on the roots of European vines, phylloxera virtually destroyed all of Europe's vines, with the exception of those growing on very sandy soils or in very cold microclimates, in which the aphid cannot survive. Phylloxera was slowly dealt with by the replanting of almost all of Italy's and Europe's vineyards on American rootstocks. The usage of American rootstocks was due to the fact that they were resistant to the aphid.

An important consequence of the phylloxera invasion was that farmers who had to replant their vineyards, often chose

Leonardo da Vinci

Leonardo (1452-1519), the internationally renowned renaissance man, had excelled in areas including invention, drawing, paint ing, sculpture, and science. In fact, his list of accomplishments is so long, his great passion for wine was relatively unknown. Having praised wine and its health benefits, referring to it as the "divine juice of the grape", Leonardo revealed his talent as a serious vintner when a vineyard in modern-day downtown Milan was offered to him by Ludovico Sforza, Duke of Milan, as payment for "The Last Supper". It was in this vineyard that the polymath maestro experimented with all parts of the winemaking process, from cultivating vines to perfecting the grape press, and even distilling brandy. A letter written in 1515 further testified to the plethora of wine knowledge Leonardo possessed, in which several pioneering methods such as fermentation in closed barrels and frequent decanting were mentioned.

"E'l vin sia temperato, poco e spesso. Non fuor di pasto, né a stomaco voto." This is the suggestion on wine drinking from Leonardo, a longtime connoisseur: "the wine should be mild, it should be drunk in small amounts, and often. Not without the meal nor on an empty stomach."

Cosimo III de' Medici

Florence is often thought of as the heart of Tuscany; a place full of masterpieces of art and rich in magnificent architecture. Wherever you visit the city, you'll run into the legacy of the famous Medici family. The family rose to power thanks to their financial business and gradually expanded their influence across the city. In 1569, the family first held the title "Grand Duchy of Tuscany", and its 6th Grand Duke, Cosimo III de' Medici established the world's oldest wine appellation.

Cosimo III de' Medici (1642-1723), Tuscany's Grand Duke, issued an edict on September 24, 1716 which delimited the wine area of four regions Chianti, Pomino, Carmignano, and Vald'Arno di Sopra, creating the first legal appellations of origin for wine in the world. The edict was so modern in its approach that it also regulated the harvest and production. Whilst more than 300 years have passed, the boundaries of these four areas remain more or less the same and the aristocratic landowners of the time, such as Antinori, Corsini, and Ricasoli who helped Cosimo III de' Medici with setting up the edict, are still well-known today as important wine producers. What an achievement by the Duke!

to do so by replanting not with the same local varieties but with new, foreign, and more resistant ones. Therefore, phylloxera is one of the major causes of the loss of grapevine biodiversity in Italy. However, Italians have become increasingly aware of how lucky they are to own absolutely unique grapevines not found anywhere else, and that allow for the production of unique, worldclass wines.

Modern Reorganisation

The modern renaissance of Italian wine really began in the 1960s, with the end of the mezzadria or sharecropping system that encouraged farmers to produce quantity rather than quality (as the more you produced the more you could keep).

From the 1960s onwards, Italian winemaking and viticulture have undergone changes more radical than in the previous three centuries combined. Matching grapevines to specific rootstocks and more suitable soils and microclimates has become commonplace; the introduction of temperature control during fermentation almost immediately upgraded the quality of Italian white wines.

Clearly, the modernisation of viticulture and winemaking led to a huge qualitative improvement in Italy's wines, first in Tuscany, Friuli-Venezia Giulia, Piedmont, and slowly spreading to all regions of the Italian peninsula. Today, it is common to hear Italian wine producers speak of the importance of carefully kept vineyards, of low yields per hectare, of the application of scientific criteria in the process of winemaking and of cellar hygiene.

Italy is one of the world's biggest exporters of wine and in fact, if the Veneto and Puglia joined together to form a new country, they would then automatically become the fourth largest wine producer in the world. This analogy explains just how much wine is made in Italy every year! However, the key thing to remember is just how broad the scope of wine being made in Italy now is. The renewed focus on native grape varieties and the drive in the international market for wines that are unique, hold a story, and are connected to a sense of place, this has given Italian producers an ideal audience that is growing year-on-year. It's no wonder that when people ask, "what's your favourite Italian wine?" that you can never choose just one!

Light white   Light red   Full-bodied white   Full-bodied red   Spumante (Sparkling)   Liquoroso (Fortified)

Camillo Benso, Conte di Cavour

Whilst Cosimo III de' Medici's edict laid the foundation for the popularity of Chianti wines in central Tuscany, up in the northwest, in Piedmont, Camillo Benso (1810-1861) was unquestionably the wine entrepreneur who brought Barolo into the spotlight. Camillo Benso, Count of Cavour, was born to a noble family in Turin and was to become a leading figure in the political movement towards Italian unification. Commonly known as Cavour, he was praised as a great statesman who took office as the first Prime Minister of Italy. In addition, Cavour gained a reputation as an adept wine entrepreneur who initiated the restyling of Barolo and paved the way for this great wine to reach the King of Sardinia's dinner table.

At the age of 22, Cavour took over the family estate and started his journey as a winery owner in Grinzane, Piedmont. He first hired Marquis Pier Francesco Staglieno as a consultant, and later entrusted the winemaking to Loui Oudar, a French oenologist, who introduced numerous changes in the vineyard and cellar, eventually leading to the dawn of modern-day Barolo wines, a dry wine made from only Nebbiolo grapes.

ADRIATIC SEA

TYRRHENIAN SEA

IONIAN SEA

Northern Italy   Central Italy   Southern Italy
                                   & the Islands

2. A JOURNEY THROUGH THE ITALIAN WINE REGIONS

NORTHERN ITALY

Italy's Northern part is composed of eight regions: Valle d'Aosta, Piedmont, Liguria, Lombardy, Veneto, Trentino-Alto Adige, Friuli-Venezia Giulia, and Emilia Romagna. The land here covers everything from the mountainous Alps, to the Ligurian and Adriatic Seas, through to the flatland of Pianura Padana. In this area it is possible to find many different grapes and many different wine styles, from the elegant and strong reds from the Langhe region, to the powerful and rich red blends from Veneto. From the fresh and aromatic wines from the Alps, to the richer and fruitier whites from the sea. The numerous sparkling wines are not to be forgotten of course, from the complex and elegant Traditional Method examples, to the lighter and easy to drink Charmat styles.

1. Valle d'Aosta

According to old legends, a Ligurian-Gallic tribe already practiced the cultivation of vines in Valle d'Aosta before 23 B.C. Today wine is still being produced in Italy's smallest and very French region – you will hear a lot of French sounding names here, for both people and places – and it is of exceptionally high-quality. Valle d'Aosta is Italy's best kept wine secret. Vineyards are often planted on terraces that help cope with the very steep gradients, indeed Valle d'Aosta's viticulture has been defined as "heroic" because of the effort that the farmer has to put forth on such difficult mountainous land, where vineyards often reach and even exceed 1,000 meters above sea level.

Valle d'Aosta, is defined by three main valleys, each of which is identified with specific wine products. The main wine production area in the region today is found on the warm and sunny slopes of the Central valley. In the Lower valley you find Donnas and the Barolo-like wine from Nebbiolo grapes, which is called Picotener in this region. In the Northern valley, the delicious Blanc de Morgex et La Salle wine is made from the native Prié Blanc variety.

2. Piedmont

Piedmont and wine are inseparable. This region has always been one of the most important wine regions of Italy. The first historical notes on grape growing here can be traced back to ancient Rome. Pliny the Elder spoke about a "spinea grape", which is probably at the origin of the name "spanna", one of the local terms often used for Nebbiolo. The key moment in the development of wine in Piedmont took place in the nineteenth century, thanks to the contributions of four personalities: Marchesa Juliette Colbert di Barolo, the oenologist Louis Oudart, Count Camillo Benso di Cavour and Gen. Paolo Francesco Staglieno. They improved the production of their wines from Piedmontese vines. It is hard to imagine that until then, Barolo was often a fizzy sweet wine, mainly as the result of poor hygiene and lack of attention in the cellars!

Most of Piedmont's wine production occurs in the hilly areas, and vineyards are mostly red grapes, with some noteworthy native and international white grapes grown as well. Temperatures in the region experience swings, both between seasons and between day and night, producing the conditions for exceptional quality wines with great complexity.

The wine-growing areas of greatest importance are: the hills of Novara and Vercelli (Northern Piedmont), with their 'Northern' Nebbiolos; the Monferrato that includes the "Astigiano" (well-known for Moscato d'Asti, and Barbera D'Asti) and "Casalese" (known for Freisa and Grignolino); the area of the Langhe and Roero, where we find the Nebbiolo wines of Barolo and Barbaresco, but also high-quality Dolcetto, Barbera and more.

Among the most cultivated native white grapes are Arneis, Cortese, and Erbaluce, but there are many more, as Piedmont is especially rich in native grapes. In addition to Nebbiolo, there are many red grape varieties grown such as Barbera, Dolcetto, Freisa, Grignolino and Brachetto, but also other varieties, ones that once risked extinction, but are having a ressurgence.

3. Liguria
Although the first accounts provided about wine in the region was given in the first century B.C., it is from the Middle Ages that we have the first reliable indications of grape growing in Liguria's key areas of Riviera di Ponente and Cinque Terre. Even from these initial reports, it is understood that growing vines in Liguria has always been very difficult, and like in Valle d'Aosta's cultivation, it is considered "heroic" because of the extremely steep mountainous slopes that plunge down into the sea below. Here we find more examples of terraced slopes, however, thanks to the influence of the sea and numerous waterways, the climate is beautifully mild. It is often difficult to find Ligurian wines outside the region due to the limited quantity produced, and the locals keeping the good stuff for themselves! The most common red grapes are Rossese

and Ormeasco (the local name for Dolcetto). Among the whites are Pigato and Vermentino, Bosco and Albarola. These last three are blended in the Cinqueterre Sciacchetrà DOC, a sweet wine made from air-dried grapes, a regional treat produced in small quantities. The Riviera di Ponente is home to the Ormeasco di Pornassio DOC and Rossese di Dolceacqua DOC, the latter probably being the best regional red wine.

4. Lombardy

That importance of wine to Lombardy is exemplified by the fact that Pavia and Brescia had already created consortiums for their wines even before the birth of the DOCs in 1963.

Lombardy is a large region characterised by many different features, from the mountainous zone in the north, to the hills, the Po Valley, and areas of Garda Lake southwards. Among the most important wine and increasingly recognised areas is Valtellina, whose vines are grown on terraces often at the limit of the maximum altitude, allowing for proper grape ripening. The main grape is Nebbiolo, here called Chiavennasca, that gives rise to both, Sforzato di Valtellina DOCG, a wine produced with the partial drying of grapes on mats (much like Amarone in Veneto), and the Valtellina Superiore DOCG.

One cannot talk of Lombardy without focusing on Franciacorta, the now world-famous sparkling wine. Produced in the same manner as Champagne from Pinot Nero, Chardonnay and Pinot Bianco. What makes these wines stand out however, is the warmer climate. Thus, Franciacorta is richer and fruitier. Although in the area of Oltrepò Pavese the most popular grape is Barbera, special mention goes to Pinot Nero, for which Oltrepò Pavese has recently established itself as a region of excellence. Here this variety is used mainly for the production of sparkling wines labelled as Oltrepò Pavese Metodo Classico DOCG.

5. Veneto

Documents from the second century B.C. report that the Romans were defeated in the Veneto thanks to the "effects" that the local wine had on the native soldiers - a powerful advert indeed! The Veneto is not only the largest producer in Italy in terms of volume, it is the region that produces the largest quantity of DOC wines in Italy. Alongside the traditional varieties typical of the Veneto; many international ones are also grown in the region, as these were heavily planted here after the phylloxera plight. The first DOC in Veneto was Lugana in 1967, followed by Bardolino, Soave, and Valpolicella.

Perhaps the most famous wines of the Veneto are the red wines of the Valpollicella DOC and of course, Amarone della Valpolicella DOCG, produced using Corvina, Rondinella, and Molinara. However, there are exceptional white wines here too. Next to the home of Valpolicella there is the beautiful hilltop town of Soave, home to wines made from Garganega. However, the two increasingly well recognised wines are actually from "interregional" DOCs, Lugana, where the white wine is made from Turbiana or the Trebbiano di Lugana grape, and Prosecco, the incredibly popular sparkling wine made from Glera.

Furthermore, the wines of the Moscato Fiori d'Arancio dei Colli Euganei DOCG made with Moscato Giallo are beginning to steal some of the limelight from other Veneto wines.

The 10 most planted grapes in Italy

Although there is a lot of focus on the "international" grape varieties planted around the world, Italy has maintained its diversity thanks to the abundance of native grape varieties. These are the 10 most planted wine grapes in Italy and all together, they represent one-third of the national vineyard area recorded as of 2017.

 **Sangiovese:** the most planted variety in Italy, this grape has many synonyms, in central Tuscany, in the town of Montalcino, it's called Brunello; while in the Scansano area, south of Tuscany, it's named Morellino.

 **Trebbiano Toscano:** it's called Ugni Blanc in France and mostly used as the base wine for distilling brandy. Trebbiano Toscano plays an important blending role in the production of many DOC and IGT wines across Italy.

 **Catarratto:** as one of the most planted white grapes, it is a blending partner to Carricante, together they make the trendy Etna Bianco DOC. It is the major grape for white wines from Alcamo DOC and Contea di Sclafani DOC.

 **Montepulciano:** another major red grape, it is not be confused with Vino Nobile di Montepulciano, the latter is a wine made from Sangiovese. Montepulciano is a versatile grape for sparkling, rose, dry and sweet reds.

Glera: the beloved grape of sparkling fans, Glera is the core of the Prosecco wine. In the centre of the premium Conegliano Valdobbiadene Prosecco DOCG, in the subzone called Cartizze is believed to produce the fuller-bodied and best Prosecco.

 **Pinot Grigio:** called Pinot Gris in its home country France, and Grauer Burgunder in Germany, it travelled to Northern Italy in the early 19th century where it got the name of Pinot Grigio. It's one of the most-exported type of varietal wine from Italy.

Merlot: is the most planted international red grape in Italy. Merlot can be made as a varietal wine in, or blended with, other grapes, to produce IGP or PDO wines. The Masseto wine from Bolgheri region could well be the most famous Italian merlot varietal wine.

Chardonnay: though varietal wines are made from Chardonnay, it's widely found in blends. Among them, the Metodo Classico sparkling wines such as Franciacorta and Trento DOC enjoy an international reputation.

Barbera: Piedmont's most planted red grape, Barbera wine is generally low in tannins, high in acidity and deep in colour. The best example could be found from Nizza DOCG and Barbera d'Asti DOCG.

Negro Amaro: Negro (black) and Amaro (*Mavros* in Latin, also meaning black) in the name indicate the dark colour of the grape. Salice Salentino DOC red is the most popular Negro Amaro wine.

6. Trentino-Alto Adige

A region of two halves, literally! Trentino-Alto Adige is composed of two autonomous provinces: Trentino in the south and Alto Adige in the north. Trentino is almost entirely Italian-speaking, while Alto Adige is predominantly German-speaking. Even the grape varieties are split here. However, there is common ground found in the warm sunbathed valleys that allow for wines much riper and richer than you'd expect from a region so far north.

Trentino

Three native red grapes are: Marzemino, Teroldego and Schiava. However, the area of Trento is home to many "international" varieties such as Pinot Gris, Pinot Noir and Cabernet. Indeed, the most cultivated white grape varieties are the international ones such as Chardonnay and Pinot Blanc, which are used with Pinot Nero in the production of classic method sparkling wine Trento DOC.

Alto Adige

Alto Adige or South-Tyrol (Süd Tirol) has vineyards that hug the mountains and foothills of the alps. Among the most commonly planted red grapes are the native Schiava (Vernatsch) and Lagrein, followed by the international Pinot Noir. The white grapes here are Gewürztraminer, Kerner and Sylvaner. Also common are Moscato Rosa and Moscato Giallo (Rosenmuskateller and Goldmuskateller), the first in the form of dessert wines of considerable thickness, the second made in both dry and sweet versions.

7. Friuli-Venezia Giulia

Whilst vines were documented in this region as early as the thirteenth and twelfth centuries B.C., the area became famous for its wines due to their trading in the Middle Ages. However, a string of bad luck with fungal diseases and phylloxera almost wiped out native vines, hence the replanting of Merlot, Cabernet Franc and Pinot Bianco grape varieties, which are now considered traditional to the area.

For the most part, Friuli-Venezia Giulia is synonymous with great white wines, especially those produced with indigenous varieties that find their perfect expression on the hills adjacent to the sea. The first DOC was Collio in 1968, followed shortly by "Colli Orientali del Friuli". Friuli-Venezia Giulia makes the some of the best white wines in the country and the most important areas for wine production are: Friuli Grave (the name derives from the pebbles that cover the ground) Collio, Colli Orientali del Friuli, Isonzo and Carso. The DOC Friuli Grave is the largest in the region representing more than half of the wine production in Friuli, whereas the DOCGs of Rosazzo, Picolit and Ramandolo provide other exceptional local wines.

8. Emilia Romagna

Although there was vine cultivation here as early as 6000 B.C., the first true vine growers were the Etruscans, who created huge expanses of vineyards in the area near Faenza. With the Middle Ages, this wine production became even more important. Over the years, it took on a key role in this region which is often referred to as the gastronomic heartland of Italy. Emilia Romagna is one of the region that has the largest wine production in Italy with Veneto, Sicily and Puglia counting about 55,000 hectares of vineyards. The first DOCG in Italy was awarded here, to the unlikely white wine of Albana di Romagna. Although considered as one region, this is another example of two areas talked about as one.

Emilia

Here, in the area of Piacenza, the most common varieties are the red grapes of Barbera and Croatina which characterise the Gutturnio DOC. The native white grape varieties of Malvasia di Candia Aromatica, and Moscato Bianco find their home here, amongst the widespread international varieties such as Chardonnay, Pinot Blanc and Pinot Gris, Riesling and Müller-Thurgau.

The areas of Reggio-Emilia and Modena are dominated by the cultivation of perhaps the best-known wine from this region: Lambrusco. Lambrusco di Sorbara and Grasparossa are most common around Modena and are the perfect wines to pair with the tortellini dishes or mortadella cold cuts famous in this area.

Romagna

In Romagna however, the most important grape is Sangiovese, which surpasses Trebbiano Romagnolo (the most common white grape variety in Romagna) in quantity. Mention must of course be given to Albana, the grape synonymous with Albana di Romagna (the first ever DOCG white wine of Italy).

CENTRAL ITALY

The central part of Italy is composed of five regions: Tuscany, Umbria, Marche, Lazio and Abruzzo. Historically famed Tuscany produces red wines from a single variety, or blended varieties of Sangiovese and Canaiolo, as well as powerful wines from international varieties such as Cabernet Sauvignon, Merlot and Cabernet Franc. In Marche, most of the notable citrusy, Riesling-like, age-worthy white wines are from Verdicchio. In the landlocked region of Umbria, the typical grapes are Grechetto for vivacious whites and tannic Sagrantino for red. Lazio is also characterised by Grechetto and shares this variety with its neighbouring region, Umbria. Lazio, together with Abruzzo, both coastal regions to the Tyrrhenian Sea and Adriatic Sea respectively, shares the dominance for Montepulciano.

9. Tuscany

Tuscany, along with Piedmont, is the region where Italy's greatest wines are considered to be made. It is a large hilly region with huge plantings and can boast many DOCGs and DOCs. Characteristic wines are from the south of Florence (Chianti and Chianti Classico), south of Siena (Montalcino and Montepulciano), and hilly coasts of Bolgheri. Whilst the temperate climate is ideal for reds, whites are also found here, such as the first ever awarded DOC of Vernaccia di San Gimignano.

Its prestige dates back to the 16th century, in fact Italy's noble wines are from this region - Montepulciano and Vernaccia di San Gimignano. the latter having been recognised as Italy's first DOC wine in 1966. The importance of this region is also reflected in having been the subject of the first vineyard zonation in Italy, as early as 1716, by the Grand Duke Cosimo Medici.

Most of Tuscany's red wines are produced using Sangiovese, Canaiolo, and Ciliegiolo. Whereas the whites are from: Trebbiano Toscano, Malvasia Bianca Lunga, Vernaccia and Ansonica.

Tuscany is the birthplace of the famous Supertuscan wines, made using mostly the international varieties of Cabernet Sauvignon, Merlot and Cabernet Franc (with some Sangiovese), these wines from the warm rolling coastal hills of Bolgheri were produced to be a rival to the great wines of Bordeaux. Although originally only allowed to be designated as an IGT, these are now some of the most prestigious and expensive wines not only in Italy, but the world.

10. Umbria

Wines were made in this region earlier than Etruscan times, and in 1549, a letter from Sante Lancerio a renaissance sommelier to the pope mentioned Pope Paul III's favourite wines including an Umbrian wine, Sucano from Orvieto.

Umbria is landlocked and hilly, and even though a small region, it has a high density of vineyards. The mountain ranges protect the vineyards from the cold winter winds, and in general it has a mild climate.

The region is best known for the Sagrantino di Montefalco DOCG made from the highly tannic Sagrantino grape. These wines are rich and powerful with fantastic ageing potential.

The region's other red grape varieties include Montepulciano, Canaiolo Nero and Ciliegiolo. Whilst the focus has historically been on Sagrantino wines, Umbria does have a native white grape: Grechetto. This is mainly found in the south of the region and the Orvieto DOC remains the region's largest accounting for an amazing 80% of wine produced. Interestingly, thanks to Lake Corbara in Orvieto, there is a microclimate that is particularly suited to the development of sweet, noble rot wines, and this is one of the few viticulture areas where noble rot occurs abundantly and frequently.

11. Marche

Whilst the Marche region was recognised in Roman times for, "Vino Piceno" a wine made from Sangiovese and Montepulciano grapes, the region has been timelessly known for is its native white grape, Verdicchio.

Marche is mostly hilly with most off its vineyards located on well situated slopes. The region benefits from the Adriatic Sea and numerous rivers that moderate temperatures for the vines. The majority of the region's plantings are Verdicchio, but there is a percentage of Montepulciano and Sangiovese.

Whilst Marche has numerous DOC and DOCGs the focus in recent years has been on those of Verdicchio del Castelli di Jesi and Verdicchio di Matelica, with these exceptional wines really putting the region on the global wine map. For red wines, the most well-known tend to be the Montepulciano and Sangiovese based blends of Conero and Rosso Piceno.

12. Lazio

Grapevines and wines in Lazio predate the arrival of the Romans. Italian poet Virgil mentions the cultivation of vines by the Sabines (the people who populated Lazio, then known as *Latium* prior to Roman invasion) in his epic work *The Aneid*. However, as the Roman Empire expanded wine became the centre of economy and daily life. After the period of phylloxera in the early 20th century, the region lost sight of quality and focused on the number of wines to produce. However, now things are getting back in shape, as winemakers have refocused on the characteristics of indigenous grapes and their ability to produce quality wines.

Most of the vineyards of Lazio are on hill slopes near to a lake. This location has a particular soil that helps contribute to the grapes' potential aroma and sugar. Whilst rain is scarce, the temperatures remain mild. Lazio's most important native grape is Cesanese which is the basis of excellent wines, such as the Cesanese d'Affile DOC and Frascati Superiore DOCG. White wines in Lazio are produced mainly using Malvasia di Lazio and Trebbiano grapes from Montefiascone, an area known for the infamous "Est! Est!! Est!!!" DOC wines.

13. Abruzzo

The wines from Abruzzo date back to the Iron age, they were massively cultivated by Etruscans and then adapted by Roman patricians!

Abruzzo is dominated by mountains and overlooks the Adriatic Sea, a positive influence that aids in moderating the region's temperature. Montepulciano is Abruzzo's king of red grapes, it represents half of the grapevines planted in the region. Indeed, the only DOCG is Montepulciano d'Abruzzo Colline Teremane. This is followed by a white grape called Trebbiano Abruzzese. Pecorino is one of the region's grapes to watch out for, with its fantastic notes of lemon drop, sage and rosemary. One must never forget to try the other DOCs, such as Cerasulo Montepulciano d'Abruzzo DOC, one of the few DOCs dedicated to rosé wines.

Top 5 PDO Wines

Sitting on the top of the quality pyramid, PDO Wines including the DOC and DOCG categories, represent the highest level of typicity and purest origin. While there are 75 DOCGs and 333 DOCs, the following 5 DOPs have the highest production figures, meaning there is a much higher chance that you will taste one of them.

Prosecco DOC

This denomination was established in the year 2009 and it covers all of the central and north-eastern Veneto and all Friuli-Venezia Giulia. Most notable as the perfect wine for aperitivos thanks to the fresh, light and lovely characteristics of the semi-sparkling (frizzante in Italian) and sparkling forms, Prosecco DOC is actually also produced in a still version. However, despite talk of adding a rosé category, Prosecco DOC remains an exclusively white wine. Glera is the main grape used for the production of Prosecco and accounts for at least 85% of the wine. A maximum of 15% Bianchetta Trevigiana, Chardonnay, Perera, Pinot Bianco, Pinot Grigio, and/or Pinot Nero (vinified as a white wine) can also be used.

Delle Venezie DOC

Also named as Pinot Grigio Delle Venezie DOC, this denomination name is self-explanatory. It spans through the Veneto, Friuli Venezia Giulia and Trentino, making up the largest Italian denomination dedicated to the Pinot Grigio grape and single variety wine, highly appreciated by consumers from the USA, UK and Germany as well as those in Italy. White wines including Bianco Delle Venezie

DOC and Pinot Grigio Delle Venezie DOC (Minimum 85% Pinot Grigio) are produced along with rosé wines, which appear copper or pink in colour depending on the pigmentation in the skins of Pinot Grigio. Semi-sparkling and sparkling wines fermented mostly with Pinot Grigio can also be found in this denomination.

By volume, this denomination contributes more than 85% of the Pinot Grigio originating from Italy, accounting for 43% of the world's total production.

Chianti DOCG

It's one of the world's most famous red wines based on Sangiovese, the noble red grape of Tuscany. The modern-day Chianti DOCG wine is a bright ruby red coloured wine, evolving into garnet with age. It is dry, savoury and slightly tannic, with scents of violet and rose petals. The production area of Chianti DOCG has been amended and expanded since the 1960s. Today, over 3,000 producers manage over 15,000 hectares of vineyard spreading around Tuscany.

The Chianti DOCG is divided into seven subzones: Chianti Rufina, Chianti Colli Aretini, Chianti Colli Fiorentini, Chianti Colli Senesi, Chianti Colline Pisane, Chianti Montalbano and Chianti Montespertoli. All the names of the subzones can appear on the label, and Chanti Rufina is the smallest but most famous, known for its robust body and racy acidity. You should not mistake Chianti Classico DOCG as a subzone of Chianti DOCG, as Chianti Classico DOCG became an independent denomination in 1996. Quite like Pinot Grigio wines, Chianti DOCG is very popular in Germany, the USA and the UK. With these three markets combined accounting for over 60% of the total export of Chianti DOCG.

Asti DOCG

This denomination covers the territories of 52 municipalities in the provinces of Asti, Cuneo, and Alessandria, in the Piemonte region. It's the realm of the Moscato Bianco grape and the wines produced in this denomination must be 100% of this aromatic variety.

Over 4000 producers work the 9700 hectares of delimited vineyards. The annual production is around 85 million bottles per year. The Traditional Method is used to produce Asti Spumante Metodo Classico (sweet), while Asti Spumante (extra dry to dolce) and Moscato d'Asti are fermented in pressurised tanks of autoclaves (Martinotti method). A late harvest dessert wine is also made here, labelled as Vendemmia Tardiva.

Notable subzones are: Canelli (Moscato d'Asti only), Santa Vittoria d'Alba (Moscato d'Asti and Vendemmia Tardiva only) and Strevi (Moscato d'Asti only).

Montepulciano d'Abruzzo DOC

The first all-region DOC of Italy, Montepulciano d'Abruzzo DOC is the flagship red wine which accounts for over 80% of total denomination wines in the Abruzzo region of east-central Italy. Made only from hilly or plateau vineyards, the altitude of which does not generally exceed 500 meters above sea level. For wines to be qualified for the DOC status, a minimum of 85% of Montepulciano is required. However, wines from the subzone Casauria require 100% Montepulciano. The wine has an intense ruby red colour and will remind you of red fruits, flowers, and spices. It's dry, soft, with a moderate level of tannins.

SOUTHERN ITALY AND THE ISLANDS

Southern Italy is composed of five mainland regions and two island regions: Molise, Campania, Puglia, Basilicata, Calabria, Sicily and Sardinia. Although traditionally thought of as simply a powerhouse of wine production that provided rich alcoholic wines for blending in the north, these regions are actually home to exceptional and complex wines in a broad range of styles. Perhaps the most surprising of these are the age-worthy white wines of Greco, Fiano and Etna Bianco which are gaining increasing recognition on the global stage.

14. Molise

There is little historical information on the historical production of wine in Molise, and indeed it is a region often overlooked in wine books! However, this tiny mostly hilly region, the second smallest in the country after Valle d'Aosta in the North, is slowly carving out a name for itself on the Italian wine map, thanks to its native grape Tintillia. A red grape that used to be known for its blending capacity, Tintillia is perhaps now more famous due to the rise in popularity (and quality) of the regional Tintilia del Molise DOC. Don't let the small size of this area fool you though, it is home to another 3 region-wide denominations, the most widely recognised being Molise DOC as well as several smaller ones, including the original in the area Biferno DOC (awarded as early as 1983), that covers both red and white wines and is named after the main river in the region.

15. Campania

Campania has been a source of fine wines since the time of the ancient Romans, and many hectares of beautiful vineyards are found within its borders. The best examples of these are located at the foot of Mount Vesuvius, on the islands of Ischia and Capri, and close to the Sorrento Peninsula. Even during the winter, the climate here is mild, providing not only an ideal tourist destination, but also long growing seasons for the grapes. The quality of its wines was recognised as early as 1966 with the awarding of the Ischia DOC. Now there are 4 DOCG, which include the well-known Greco di Tufo and Taurasi wines, and 20 DOCs. As well as being home to Aglianico, the red grape variety used in the Taurasi DOCG, you will also find Piedirosso in Campania which is often blended with Aglianico to help soften the tannins and produce easier drinking styles of wine. Whilst the white grape Greco might be best known from this region, Falanghina and Fiano are both grown here too and produce exceptional wines in a range of styles.

16. Puglia

Grape growing in Puglia goes back as far as 2000 B.C., earlier than the arrival of the Phoenician merchants, and even Horace was writing about how delicious the wines of Taranto were! There are large areas of flat land in Puglia making it perfect not only for vineyards, but all sorts of other farming. The soils here are rich, but rainfall is limited and the blue skies and sunshine typical of the Mediterranean are found throughout the year. These perfect conditions mean that Puglia is responsible for around one third of all wine production in Italy.

Whilst Puglia is best known for red grape varieties such as Primitivo, Uva di Troia and Negro Amaro, you might be surprised to learn that many white grapes also thrive in these warm, dry conditions. In particular here you find Malvasia Bianca, Minutolo, Fiano and Bombino Bianco. These grapes characterise the local DOC wines, among which Primitivo di Manduria DOC (and the recent DOCG Primitivo di Manduria Dolce Naturale) and the wines of the DOC Salice Salentino can be counted, both of which have gained significant renown both in Italy and abroad.

17. Basilicata

Today Basilicata is mainly known for its red wine production, and wines such as Aglianico del Vulture for example, are always dry, and of especially high quality (in 1971, Aglianico del Vulture obtained the region's first DOC). This description however, is a stark contrast to what historians wrote concerning this region in the 1620s, back then, Basilicata was famed as producing "sweet, fragrant and golden" wines, this is quite the turnaround!

A region that is more than 80% hills and mountains, it is particularly suited to quality grape production, not least because of its varied soils. Like Campania, it is also home to an extinct volcano, the Vulture. Here grapes grow both in the foothills and up to 700 meters above sea level. This gives excellent opportunities for a shift between day and night temperature, a condition that increases complexity and flavour development in grapes and helps to maintain refreshing acidity in wines found in warmer regions.

The most important area is in the province of Potenza where the Aglianico grape is grown and that also characterises Basilicata's only DOCG area: Aglianico del Vulture Superiore DOCG.

18. Calabria

Another of the truly ancient southern regions of grape production. The Greeks called the people of what is now Calabria, *Enotri*, for their care and skill in the cultivation of the vine, and then, somewhat ironically, helped them improve growing methods! However, like Molise, it is a region that has often been overlooked by those both inside and outside of Italy.

With almost half of the area covered in mountains, vines find few areas to grow here, and in stark contrast to a large area such as Puglia, grapes in Calabria represent only 3% of farming production. Originally known for the production of high alcohol, intensely coloured wines that were used for blending, Calabria has slowly been changing its image, helped by an increased focus on Gaglioppo, the red grape that finds its home here and dominates in the Cirò DOC, as well as many of the other wines produced here. When not drinking wines made from Gaglioppo, you could encounter other red grapes such as Nerello Mascalese, Nerello Cappuccio or Magliocco. In fact, red wines account for 80% of the production in Calabria.

White wines are dominated by Greco Bianco, especially those likely to be imported from the region. These are found in dry styles however, there is a dedicated denomination for these Greco di Bianco wines, which represents an interesting and delicious dessert wine!

19. Sicily

Historically, Sicily's most famous wine was Mamertino, a favourite of Julius Caesar – so this region has always gotten good press! Interestingly, it was a Brit who featured prominently in the success of wine from Sicily in the first part of modern history; in the eighteenth century, John Woodhouse, a merchant who used to send dry "white wine of Marsala" to England by fortifying it with alcohol to help it keep during the voyage, started modern day Marsala wine production. This really put the island on the map in a period when the rest of Sicilian wine was mainly used for blending purposes.

Sicily is such a large landmass, that it is hard to characterise in a simple fashion, each quarter is defined by different characteristics, from the sea breezes of areas that hug the coast, to the altitude found in the Etna region, and then the large warm central areas. Let's not forget the volcanic Pantelleria and Aeolian islands. In fact, the main island is so large that the vineyard area is among the largest in Italy, indeed it's 15% larger than Puglia's.

The only Sicilian DOCG is Cerasuolo di Vittoria DOCG, made with a blend of Frappato and Nero d'Avola grapes in an area close to the south coast. There is also a DOC here, called simply Vittoria DOC which also includes white wines made mainly with the grape Inzolia.

Whilst Ceresualo di Vittoria is the DOCG, most people actually know Sicily thanks to the rise in popularity of the wines from the Etna DOC. Found on the slopes surrounding the Etna volcano, these wines are defined by strong mineral characters and are produced both in red made from blending Nerello Mascalese and Nerello Cappuccio, and also white from primarily Carricante. The Faro DOC is also worth mentioning, in the province of Messina, this was one of the first in Sicily and produces highly promising wines based on Nerello Mascalese, Nerello Cappuccio and Nocera.

It is not just great dry wines that are found on this expansive Island. Sicily is the home to many great sweet wines: Malvasia delle Lipari produced from grapes Malvasia di Lipari and Corinto Nero; Moscato di Siracusa and Moscato di Noto from Moscato Bianco grapes; Moscato di Pantelleria from Zibibbo or Moscato di Alessandria, and of course, was first made famous by the fortified wines produced in the Marsala DOC. These are based on the white grapes Grillo, Cararratto and Ansonica (often locally referred to as Inzolia), or for the production of ruby wines, for which producers use Perricone, Nero d'Avola or even Nerello Mascalese.

20. Sardinia

The island of Sardinia has a long and varied history of wine, and its position in the Mediterranean has made it a target for many conquering forces. Whilst the Phoenicians led the interest in winemaking and grape growing here, it was fall of the Byzantine Empire that brought fame to the region. In modern history, the first DOC, the Vernaccia di Oristano DOC was awarded in 1971. Yet despite this, for many years Sardinian wines were not particularly popular due to their reputation for being full-bodied but with little in the way of acidity, and considerable alcohol. Fortunately, the last 30 years have seen great strides to improve quality and techniques, and now Sardinian wines are becoming increasingly popular and recognised around the world. In terms of wine, the island is not defined by its coastline, but actually by the hills and characteristic sand or granite soils that have significant impact on the styles of the wines. It can be very hot and windy here, with little rainfall, helping to produce concentrated wines. The most cultivated red grapes include Cannonau, Monica, Carignano, Pascale and Bovale, while Nuragus, Vermentino and Malvasia di Sardegna are the main white grapes. The only DOCG is Vermentino di Gallura.

There are 18 DOCs, amongst them Vernaccia di Oristano (DOC), made of the native Vernaccia di Oristano grape, is of great interest. This is a wine that can be aged for two years in barrels, with a minimum alcoholic strength of 14%, and as well as dry styles, there is also a fortified version, or liquoroso style. It is increasingly becoming the "must try" wine from Sardinia.

Italian Grapes around the World

Whilst Pinot Grigio has long been considered a "international" variety, you might be surprised to find many Italian native grape varieties have travelled the world and found their home in some unusual places.

1. **California:** Barbera, Sangiovese, Nebbiolo, Arneis, Dolcetto, Malvasia, Friulano, Sagrantino
2. **Texas:** Sangiovese, Vermentino
3. **Washington:** Sangiovese
4. **Long Island NY:** Friulano, Ribolla Gialla, Lagrein and Refosco
5. **Virginia:** Nebbiolo

6. **Argentina:** Nebbiolo
7. **Brazil:** Glera, Nebbiolo
8. **New Zealand:** Arneis, Montepulciano
9. **Australia:** Nero d'Avola, Arneis, Barbera,
   Nebbiolo, Sangiovese, Fiano, Aglianico, Vermentino
10. **South Africa:** Barbera, Nebbiolo, Sangiovese
    and Primitivo, Vermentino, Nero d'Avola

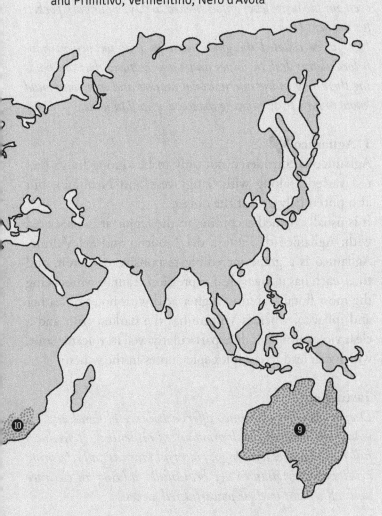

3. 55 ITALIAN VARIETIES YOU SHOULD TRY

Italy has so many native grape varieties, that we think people might have stopped counting once they got to around 600! It's hard to narrow this list down, in fact there were many arguments in the authors' meetings and some of us had to admit that even our favourite lesser grapes needed to stay in our back pockets for the next book.

Here we've collated the grape varieties that we believe have helped define Italian wines and wine culture, that are holding their own in the international market and that you should know to start truly enjoying the scope of Italian wine.

1. Aglianico 🍇

Aglianico is considered not only to be among Italy's best red varieties along with Sangiovese and Nebbiolo, but also potentially one of the oldest.

It is usually named according to the region it is associated with: Aglianico di Taurasi, del Taburno and del Vulture. Aglianico is a grape incredibly responsive to terroir, and thus, each has its own clear expression. Taurasi wines being the most floral, Taburno higher acid with notes of leather and tobacco, whereas Vulture has the darkest fruit and a clear violet aroma. It does particularly well in volcanic soils, which can lead to complex spicy notes in the wines.

Tasting note
Deeply coloured, Aglianico offers a balance of floral and savoury aromas along with pronounced minerality. It produces full-bodied wines with high, powerful tannins and refreshing acidity. Most Aglianico age beautifully, adding an elegance and refinement to these powerful red wines.

2. Albana 🍇

The grape behind the first white denomination that was bestowed DOCG status in 1987 is Albana di Romagna. (The name was changed to Romagna Albana DOCG in 2011). It is most likely named after its white colour (from Latin *albus* meaning white). It is present in Emilia Romagna and is used for Romagna Albana DOCG, Romagna DOC. In general, the still dry wines are less exciting than its sweet wines, which can range from off-dry late harvest, to luscious air-dried dessert ones.

Tasting note
Albana's wines are full-bodied and structured such that they almost resemble a red wine, showing notes of honey, exotic tropical fruits and ripe pears. However, its tannic nature also means that it oxidizes easily.

3. Arneis 🍇

Nearly extinct half a century ago, Arneis has become an iconic white grape thanks to the almost overnight success of Ceretto's Blangé bottling, launched in the 1980s. It's one of the most important white grapes in Piedmont, used for Roero DOCG Arneis, and the Langhe DOC. Before it became popular as a dry still white wine, Arneis was usually made into a sweet wine. Historically, a small dose of Arneis was used to soften the high acidity of Nebbiolo and Barbera wines.

Tasting note
Pale straw yellow in colour with low to medium acidity (this is why Arneis is rarely, if ever, used to make sparkling wines). The best wines are fresh and lively, exuding notes of fresh white

peach and pear with nuances of sweet almond and white flowers. As Arneis oxidizes easily, care must be taken during winemaking to reduce oxygen contact in order to retain its freshness.

4. Barbera

Among Italy's top 10 most planted grape varieties, Barbera is cultivated in just about every region in Italy. Several theories abound on the origin of the name Barbera, one plausible story being that it derives from the word *barbarus* (the Latin term for "foreign" or "savage") due to it dark, savage colour. Mainly grown in Piedmont, large plantings are also found in Lombardy, Emilia Romagna and Sardinia. It is widely held that the highest expressions come from Piedmont, in particular, the areas around Alba, Asti and Alessandria. Main DOCs are Barbera d'Asti DOCG, Nizza DOCG, Barbera del Monferrato Superiore DOCG, Barbera d'Alba DOC, Barbera del Monferrato DOC, Oltrepò Pavese DOC and Gutturnio DOC. Used mainly to produce dry and still reds, nowadays the majority are typically monovarietal bottlings, but examples do exist of Barbera blended with other local varieties and occasionally international grapes. Oaked versions often show a fuller mouthfeel and higher tannins.

Tasting note
Styles vary widely, from light and moderately interesting, to serious and red fruit driven, to big, oaky tannic versions that boast notes of chocolate and vanilla. Regardless, the hallmarks of the variety are a deep ruby-purple colour, very moderate tannins, red and black cherry and fruit, hints of underbrush and last but not least, its unmistakable high acidity that make it such a food-friendly option.

Appellation Explained (DOC, DOCG, IGT)

The essential components of Italian wine classification are origin and typicity. There are several levels of certification, and the higher the level, the more it guarantees. A consortium body in Italy tests the wine's standard for designation eligibility (e.g. DOC or DOCG). The European Union divides wines into three main categories. In 1987 the EU released a regulation that provided protocols for wine production and its regulation, within which, it gave specific instructions regarding production area, grape varieties, viticulture, winemaking, labelling and wine characteristics.

A *Disciplinare di Produzione* (production protocol) is a series of guidelines that qualifies wine for DOP and IGP categories. Designations of Origin and Protected Geographical Indications are reserved for wine products that comply with the conditions laid down in 2010. The illustration below shows the hierarchy of Italian wines in terms of quality. The pyramid considers both quantity and quality. The higher the quality, the lesser the total quantity available, since law regulates the maximum quantity of grapes per hectare, commonly referred to as yield. In terms of law control, it also designates quality by identifying places of origin directly linked to the quality wine hierarchy. The law has set the general guidelines based on the connections between wine and territory.

Vino da Tavola

Many of the wines in the initial category, common table wines, can become exceptional wines thanks to the

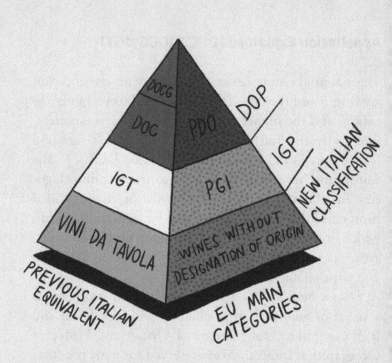

scope for experimentation. As regulations are not very strict, this category has the broadest possibility for innovation.

Indicazione Geografica Tipica (IGT)
As the level climbs higher, the guidelines become tighter. Indicazione Geografica Tipica or IGT wines are characterised by a broad indication of geographic area of origin, although, basic vineyard and vintage are not a legal requirement and can be opted out from the label. Up to 80% of grapes must come from the geographic area; passing a resemblance to the historically produced wines by the region (as by the word 'tipico' or typical). The IGT category allows for some innovation and pres-

ence of new exciting wines, while the DOC and DOCG wines safeguard tradition. The Italian Ministry of Agriculture holds a database of DOC and DOCGs. DOC was instituted in 1963 and modelled after France's Apellation d'Origine Controllée.

Denominazione di Origine Controllata (DOC)

Denominazione di Origine Controllata or DOC wines ideally remain faithful to the historical wine style of the indicated area. To be able to qualify for DOC, wineries must follow an extremely detailed set of requirements provided by the disciplinary protocols approved by a ministerial decree. A DOC wine must have formally held an IGT classification for the past five years, and at least 35% of the area's total producers have made wines in the previous 2 years, representing 35% of the production area. Other merits can also be added by the government committee.

Denominazione di Origine Controllata e Garantita (DOCG) Wines

Denominazione di Origine Controllata e Garantita or DOCG is the highest category in the classification system. It is reserved for wines that were DOC wines in the previous 10 years, with at least 51% of the area's total wine production volume. To qualify for this category, wineries must comply to an even narrower criteria: smaller production area, lower yields, and stricter rules on winemaking. After thorough laboratory tests and tastings, nomination is given by the Chamber of Commerce. The surveillance is high to deter any attempts to forge DOCG wines.

5. Canaiolo 🍇

This used to be the main Chianti grape back in the 16th century. Now, it plays a marginal role in the Tuscan blend. It shouldn't be confused with Canaiolo Nero in Umbria (these are Colorinos) or the Canaiola in north-western Lazio. Tuscany is the spotlight for this grape variety. It can be found in DOCGs and DOCs in this region; namely, Chianti DOCG, Chianti Classico DOCG, Vino Nobile di Montepulciano DOCG, Rosso di Montepulciano DOC and Carmignano DOCG. Whilst it is rare to find as a single varietal, they are increasingly being bottled and are worth hunting out.

Tasting note
Canaiolo wines have a lifted red berry and sour red cherry character, it is used in in many Tuscan blends to soften Sangiovese's tannins and enhance its drinkability.

6. Cannonau 🍇

Sardinia's signature red grape, Cannonau is identical to France's Grenache and Spain's Garnacha. In fact, this grape appears in many guises, both across Italy and around the world. However, those worth hunting out to try include the Cannonau di Sardegna DOC wines, especially those in the cru area of Jerzu, as well as the interesting and unusual expression found as Colli del Trasimeno in Umbria and in Riviera Ligure di Ponente DOC Granaccia in Liguria.

Tasting note
These wines are classically characterised by aromas of red berries (strawberry and raspberry) as well as, floral and herbal

notes. This is a very adaptive variety however, and therefore, examples across the country vary, for example those made in Sardinia and Veneto tend to be fruitier and more intense than those made in Umbria.

7. Carricante 🍇

While Carricante used to be cultivated throughout Sicily, it is now essentially confined to Mount Etna where it accounts for 95% of white grapes grown, and of course its increasing success is due to the worldwide renown of the Etna Bianco DOC. It can withstand extremely high altitudes and has extremely high acid which aids both late harvesting and age worthiness.

Tasting note

Carricante gives wines that are low in alcohol and high in acid. Refined, pure and racy, it offers flavours of lemon, aniseed, green apple, orange flower, chamomile and unripe apricot. Old vines impart added depth and complexity as well as a palpable salinity and minerality. Often described as a dry Riesling lookalike, it develops flint and diesel aromas with 5 to 10 years of age and it is one of the few Italian whites that ages well.

8. Catarratto 🍇

Italy's second most common white variety and it is somewhat unexpectedly related to Garganega from the north of Italy; often blended, it can be found in the Marsala and Menfi DOCs, as well as the regionwide Sicilia DOC. If this vine is planted on hillsides, acidity can be maintained while helping to develop more intense aromas and flavours.

9. Cesanese

This variety is used for three important wines in Lazio, Cesanese del Piglio DOCG, Cesanese di Olevano Romano DOC and Cesanese d'Affile DOC. This is known to be a grape that works well in vineyards here and planted all over the region.

10. Cortese

As the grape behind the wines of Gavi, Cortese was fashionable in the 1960s and 1970s, but lost favour in the 1980s due to too many neutral, tart, thin examples. Many young dynamic producers have recently turned their attention to this elegant grape and are restoring it to its former glory. It is found in the northern regions, particularly in Piedmont, in the Gavi DOCG, Piemonte DOC Cortese, Cortese dell'Alto Monferrato DOC; in Lombardy, in Oltrepò Pavese DOC Cortese and in Veneto in Garda DOC Cortese, Bianco di Custoza DOC. It is almost always made in a dry, crisp style. While there are some experiments with oak to tame the acidity, it quickly overwhelms Cortese's delicate expression. High acidity lends Cortese to sparkling wine production.

Tasting note

Cortese demonstrates fairly neutral aromas. It is lemony with delicate white flowers and herbal nuances and always sports high acidity. The best examples are mineral and age-worthy, while those from high yielding vines are insipid and lack interest.

11. Corvina

The most important grape variety in the wines of Valpolicella, Corvina translates as little raven. Either the dark colour of the grapes is reminiscent of the raven's plumage or it refers to the raven's attraction to the grapes when they are ripe. In the Veneto it is used to produce Valpolicella DOC, Valpolicella Ripasso DOC, Amarone della Valpolicella DOCG, Recioto della Valpolicella DOCG, Bardolino DOC, Bardolino Superiore DOCG, and the Verona IGP. Amongst the dry wines, Bardolino and Valpolicella are characterised by light to medium-bodied reds made from fresh grapes, while Amarone della Valpolicella is a full-bodied, rich, high alcohol red made from air-dried grapes. Valpolicella Ripasso is made by adding the unpressed skins of Amarone to Valpolicella which encourages a second fermentation, increasing the alcohol by a couple of degrees and giving the wine extra weight. Recioto della Valpolicella is a sweet counterpart to Amarone. Finally, Bardolino Chiaretto is among Italy's finest rosatos.

What's in a name?
Learning the label lingo!

Italy began developing its official wine classifications in the 1960s. The DOC and DOCG categories were introduced in 1963, and the IGT category followed in the early 1990s, and since then, this information has been proudly displayed on Italian labels. In addition, Italian wines are required to show certain basic information (producer name, appellation, vintage, alcohol content and bottle volume) by law. Yet, despite this degree of standardisation, Italian wine labels are widely varied in how they look. Fortunately, there are always clues that you can use to help you determine what's in the bottle.

The next time you are looking bewildered at an Italian wine label, try to identify the following things first, as this might begin to point you in the right direction for what you want.

• **Wine Type:** this can often be identified by the region or sub-region and will always be located next to the classification level, (DOCG, DOC, IGT, Vino da Tavola). If you're lucky you might even spot the grape variety – but like many other European's, the Italians often expect you to just know what it will be.

• **Producer Name:** Italian wineries will often use words like *Tenuta, Azienda, Castello or Cascina* in their name that is usually the family name. Producers often have more than one wine and aspire to a house style, therefore if you've liked one of their wines before and recognise the name it's often worth trying their others.

• **Vintage:** whilst you may not know that 2010 was the "vintage of the decade" the year of the wine can be helpful in other ways. For example, do you really want a white that is six years old, or do you fancy a young fresh red wine? Younger wines will tend to be fruiter and fresher, older wines might have more powerful flavours of oak or oxidation. Even though this is of course a huge generalisation it could help you select what you're in the mood for drinking.

• **Alcohol:** again, whilst rarely a criterion by which to solely select your wine, you will know if you fancy a big powerful mouth-filling 14.5% wine, or a gentler 12%.

In addition to this information, Italy has other wine categories that are meant to be helpful for customers. These terms are established only for DOC and DOCG wines and aim to help consumers identify specific characteristics in relation to production zone, alcohol content, ageing potential and more. These terms are used on the labels when a wine meets specific requirements and thus, can help if you happen to remember their meaning. These terms are: Riserva (Reserve), Superiore (Superior) and Classico (Classic) or Storico (Historical) - the less commonly used variant.

12. Croatina 🍇

Croatina is the subject of much confusion as in some regions it is referred to as Bonarda (which is a different grape altogether). Local synonyms include Nebbiolo di Gattinara and Spanna di Ghemme. Not the same as any of the Bonarda something grapes (eg. Bonarda Piemontese, Bonarda Novarese). Planted in most parts of north Italy, it can be found in Lombardy in Bonarda dell'Oltrepò Pavese DOC; Piedmont in Colline Novaresi DOC Croatina, Emilia Romagna in Colli Piacentini DOC Bonarda, Gutturnio DOC, and it is also grown in the Veneto and Sardinia. Croatina is typically used for dry wines, though historically it was made with a bit of residual sugar to balance out the high tannins.

13. Dolcetto 🍇

Decreasing plantings in the Langhe are due to the rise in plantings of Nebbiolo, as well as the viticultural and wine-making difficulties that Dolcetto poses. Dolcetto's grapes are quite sweet and local farmers often ate them as table grapes, thus giving rise to its nickname "little sweet one", however, its wines are always dry. In Liguria it is found under the name Ormeasco. The main DOCs in Piedmont are Dogliani DOCG, Diano d'Alba DOCG, Dolcetto d'Alba DOC, Dolcetto d'Asti DOC, and Dolcetto d'Acqui DOC. Whereas Ormeasco di Pornassio DOC is the important wine in Liguria.

Tasting note
Dazzling purple hues. Relatively low in acid and high in tannins with truly grapey aromas and flavours. Red fruits – raspberries, cherries – are often heightened by a hint of lavender, and rounded out with orange peel and black tea. Usually this grape is used for dry, still, medium-bodied red wines and it is almost always monovarietal.

14. Erbaluce

Little-known outside of northern Piedmont, this wine has a distinguished past, including having its wines win gold at the Paris Exhibition of 1855, the very same fair that yielded the famous 1855 classification of Bordeaux's Medoc and Sauternes wines. Legend has it that a fairy called Albaluce (dawn's light) bestowed the variety on the people of Caluso as a gift, and the name of the variety has morphed into Erbaluce. Dry and still is the most common style; also made into sparkling and/or sweet wines, both late-harvested and air-dried. This variety is virtually never blended and oaked examples are uncommon. The passito wines from air dried Erbaluce, though rare, can fascinate with elements of honey, fig, almond and even tropical notes, unusual for wines grown at this latitude. It's used in Erbaluce di Caluso/Caluso DOCG, Canavese DOC, Colline Novaresi DOC, Coste della Sesia DOC.

Tasting note
Pale lemon with green tinges. The grape's high acidity results in very fresh, crisp, mineral-driven wines. Aromas include white flowers, nuances of apricot, and very faint notes of green grass. All around delicate wines.

15. Falanghina
Considered to be among Campania's oldest varieties. Falanghina tends to be separated into two types, those from Flegrea, which are floral, and those from Beneventana which are more structured and often have more alcohol. Look out particularly for the wines of Falanghina del Sannio DOC which offer some of the best expressions.

Tasting note
These are wines with high acidity, floral aromas and sometimes a pungent leafy green note. On the palate, stone fruits such as peach and apricot combine with a characteristic yellow apple note to yield wines that are full of flavour. In the best examples the fruit and floral components are backed by a distinct mineral streak and a palpable texture. Due to its high acidity, there are producers experimenting with sparkling wines, watch this space!

16. Fiano
Saved from oblivion in 1945 by Mastroberardino's first varietal bottling, Fiano is arguably one of Italy's greatest white grape varieties, particularly those from the Fiano di Avelli-

no DOCG and the cru of Lapio. Like Aglianico, and many of the other grapes from the south, its affinity with volcanic soils is clear and gives a rich smokey character to some wines which match perfectly with its aromatic potential.

Tasting Note

The wine is pale yellow, though often with a green tinge. It can range from lean and mineral to rich and full-bodied, with notes of white blossoms, pear, green apple and a pleasant hint of hazelnut. They can be remarkably age-worthy and with time can take on notes of beeswax and acacia honey, becoming creamier and even oily on the palate.

17. Frappato

One of Sicily's oldest grape varieties, responsible for some of her most delicious wines, both as a single varietal and as part of a blend. The most famous of the latter of course being the Cerasuolo di Vittoria DOCG. Frappato is a grape well suited to hot and dry conditions and the red sandy-calcareous soil around Vittoria is the best for giving refined fragrant wines.

Tasting note

Frappato has a light, pale red colour and has low tannins and moderate alcohol. This results in a fresh and juicy medium-bodied wine that is fragrant with notes of strawberries and dried herbs. It is particularly pleasurable when served lightly chilled.

18. Freisa

Though historically popular, today Freisa is unfashionable with wine drinkers prompting many growers to replant with other grape varieties. The name comes from the Latin *fresia*, meaning strawberry due to its strawberry-like aromas. Usually dry and still, it can sometimes also be made as a sparkling. Some producers try to tame Freisa's tannins by making the wine frizzante (lightly fizzy) using carbon dioxide (CO_2) to neutralise the tannic mouthfeel. It is used in Freisa d'Asti DOC, Langhe DOC Freisa, Piemonte DOC Freisa.

Tasting note

Freisa is generally light and pale in colour. It is fairly rustic and can be very reductive at first. However, as it opens up, Freisa demonstrates strong scents of strawberries, and when very ripe, rose, tobacco and violet. On the palate, flavours of crisp strawberry and sour red cherry are supported by palate-cleansing acid and high tannins which lend ageability (though the tannins can be bitter and hard).

19. Fumin

The most cultivated red grape in the central part of Valle d'Aosta. Its thick white bloom, which looks powdered with ash (*fumo* in Italian) gave rise to the name Fumin. Fumin is related to two other important local varieties, as the progenitor of Vuillermin and as the sibling of Petit Rouge. It can be found in the Valle d'Aosta DOC labelled specifically as Fumin.

Tasting note

This medium-weight wine has a red fruit dominant flavour profile with nuances of smoky spices, black pepper and a green herbal undertone. With good colour, firm acidity and solid tannic structure, it has reasonable ageing potential.

20. Gaglioppo

One of the most ancient varieties. Some believe it was the wine made by the ancient Greeks that was served as a reward to Olympic game winners – what lucky athletes! Gaglioppo finds its etymological roots in a Greek word meaning "beautiful foot" and is actually a natural crossing between Sangiovese and Mantonico. Although Gaglioppo can easily earn the title of being one of the most challenging grapes to grow and vinify, it is worth persevering with and its best expressions are found in the Ciro DOC.

Tasting note

Its pale and delicate, light orangey hue is rather pretty in the glass and the best varietal versions smell and taste of small red berries and pomegranate, with an undertone of minerals and dried herbs.

21. Garganega

One of Italy's oldest and most important grapes, Garganega is the grape responsible for the world-famous Soave, among the earliest documented wines in Italy. In the Soave DOC, the wines can be, but are not necessarily, made with 100% Garganega. Recioto di Soave DOCG (rich, honeyed and floral) and Recioto di Gambellara DOCG (mineral and slightly oxidative) are sweet whites made from air-dried grapes, traditionally without botrytis, though this has recently become more common. Called Grecanico Dorato in Sicily, it can be found as a dry white monovarietal but is commonly blended with grapes like Inzolia and Chardonnay and can be found in the Alcamo DOC, among others.

Tasting note

Ripe fruit, hay and floral notes are typical. A well-made, unoaked Garganega is steely and minerally, with white flowers, apricot, citrus, and yellow apple aromas and flavours. The finest are complex and age-worthy.

22. Glera

The grape of Prosecco, Glera was known for a long time as Prosecco, but that name should now be used exclusively for the wine. These wines can be made as a still or frizzante white wine, but almost all is spumante. Extra dry is the normal sweetness level, but sweeter as well as brut versions are also common. The main denominations are Prosecco DOC, Conegliano Valdobbiadene Prosecco DOCG, and Asolo Prosecco DOCG.

Tasting note

These wines are characterised by being lightly aromatic, with aromas and flavours of buttercup, green apple, pear and white peach.

23. Grechetto

The name is derived from the fame of Greek wines of ancient Rome. Often when speaking of "Grechetto" people are actually referring to two unrelated varieties, often blended together - Grechetto di Orvieto and Grechetto di Todi (aka Pignoletto). The latter is most likely related to Trebbiano, thus, it is better not to refer to it simply as Grechetto.

These wines are found in both Emilia Romagna and Umbria. They key Umbria DOC of Orvieto must have a minimum of 60% Grechetto and/or Trebbiano Toscana. Traditionally, Orvieto produces a late-harvest noble rot wine from this grape. The notable DOCG is found in Emilia Romagna, the Colli Bolognesi Pignoletto DOCG.

Tasting note

Generally still and dry, the wine has a quaffable citrus scent indicating notes of white blossoms, green apple and pear. This vivacity is complimented by its acidity. Botrytis examples from Umbria can be complex with savoury notes of almonds and hints of orange marmalade.

24. Grignolino

Wines made from Grignolino were once highly prized by Piemontese nobility and even commanded similar prices to Barolo. The name derives from *grignolé* a word in the Piemontese dialect, which means grimace. Alternatively, the word means pips, alluding to the greater number of pips it has in comparison with other grape varieties. Usually it is dry and still, with no oak, however, some producers are experimenting with barrel ageing. Found mainly in Piedmont in the Grignolino del Monferrato Casalese DOC, and Piemonte DOC Grignolino.

Tasting note

Very pale red, almost pink in colour often with a garnet or orange hue. Colour is difficult to extract but longer macerations result in bitter, astringent tannins. Grignolino charms with perfumed aromas such as sour red cherry, red currant, iris, rosehip and white pepper. On the palate; crunchy acid and mouth-scrubbing, high tannins frame sinewy rather than rich fruit. Grignolino is always light in body and typically very moderate in alcohol.

Look Into the Origin and Authenticity

Classico

Classico (Classic), for DOC and DOCG wines or Storico (Historical), for DOCG and DOC sparkling wines, refer to wines from the historical heartland of production that are known to have been associated with quality wine production for a long time. An example is the difference between Chianti, produced in a vast area of Tuscany, and Chianti Classico, produced instead, in the small area that historically has been the epitome of this wine. Other examples can be found in Valpolicella Classico, Orvieto Classico, Verdicchio Castello di Jesi Classico and Soave Classico. All of these wines, plus their counterparts from other regions should, in theory, be more concentrated, complex and in fact a more "classic" example of the style.

Riserva

The Riserva (Reserve) qualification is found in many DOCG and DOC wines. The Riserva label is attributed to wines with a minimum ageing period of no less than two years for red wines, and no less than one year for white wines. This is a term that is equally applicable to sparkling, indeed, aged no less than one year for sparkling wines, or three years for those specifically produced with secondary refermentation in the bottle. These are of course only guidelines and many wines labelled as Riserva actually have a much longer ageing period. Often, these wines may have higher alcohol than non-Riserva wines, and sometimes this is even required by law.

In simpler terms, a Riserva wine almost always refers to one of better quality and is aged for a longer amount of time in oak (usually one additional year). As the wine was supposedly made from higher quality grapes and is richer and more concentrated than the non-Riserva wine, it ought to be able to withstand time and benefit from more time in oak. Be wary though, as with all terms, this is simply a suggestion and some Riserva wines are just overly oaked and lacking fruit.

Superiore

This qualification is very similar to the previous one. Superiore (Superior) is also a term given to DOC and DOCG wines to indicate a higher alcohol content and a mandatory minimum ageing. In fact, the Superiore guidelines adhere to the same laws as the Riserva ones. There could also be a requirement not only for a longer ageing period, but a lower grape yield per hectare than those mandated for generic wine. It is important to mention however that the Superiore qualification cannot be used for those already carrying Riserva or Novello labels. Examples of Superiore wines include: Barbera d'Asti Superiore, Barbera d'Alba Superiore, Valtellina Superiore, Frascati Superiore, and more. You know, in Italy, everyone wants to be Superiore!

Novello

Novello is a term for both still and sparkling wines that cannot be released for consumption before 00.01AM on the sixth day of November, in the year the grapes were grown. Novello is the equivalent of France's Nouveau term. These wines must contain at least 30% of wine produced through whole grape carbonic maceration, with a minimum alcohol content of 11% and with the vintage year on the label. Unfortunately, a minimum carbonic maceration requirement of 30% is much too low to truly show off what these wines could be at their best - a real shame, for Italy has the potential to make truly outstanding Novello wines. The best examples are probably those made in Trentino and Alto Adige, though, as always, there are very fine exceptions from other regions as well.

Passito or Vino Passito
These are the words for IGT, DOC and DOCG sweet wines made from grapes that are dried either naturally or in a controlled environment before they are fermented. A fortified version of this category also exists - Vino Passito Liquoroso. Note that few people in Italy, even those who write about wines, have much of an understanding of the differences between late harvest and air-dried wines, and often use the names interchangeably to describe a sweet wine generically. As you will soon discover upon trying these wines, it is not accurate, as the two processes and the styles they produce are startlingly different. Important examples of these styles include, Passito di Pantelleria DOC as a passito, and Marsala DOC and Vin Santo del Chianti DOC as a liquoroso style.

25. Grillo

Grillo is making a comeback and is now considered one of Sicily's highest quality varieties. It is not named after a cricket (*grillo*) but comes from *grilli*, the Sicilian word for pips. Being very heat and drought tolerant, Grillo is well suited to Sicily and is most often seen as a single varietally labelled Sicilia DOC wine.

Tasting note

Modern winemaking has made a big impact on Grillo's expression as it is ideally suited to reductive winemaking. This is increasingly the most popular global style, resulting wines are lemony and herbal with crisp acidity and often resemble Sauvignon Blanc. However, like Carricante it is also a key part of the Marsala blend.

26. Lagrein

Lagrein is the most important red grape variety of Alto Adige and that region's native answer to Cabernet Sauvignon. The name comes, most likely, from Vallagarina, a valley in Trentino. It is related to Teroldego and possibly to Marzemino, Schiava Gentile, Pinot Nero, and/ or Syrah. Usually used to produce dry, still red or rosato, Lagrein's DOCs are Alto Adige/Südtirol DOC, Trentino DOC and the Valdadige/Etschtaler DOC.

Tasting note

Very high in anthocyanins and therefore very dark in colour. It is full-bodied and tannic, with dark berry fruit flavours and a bitter finish.

27. Marzemino 🍇

A grape which Mozart greatly admired. Marzemino is proven to be the offspring of Teroldego, and a parent of Marzemina Bianca and Refosco del Peduncolo Rosso. It is found in the DOC of Trentino Marzemino; it is mostly planted around the area of Vallagarina and the towns of Rovereto and Isera; Ziresi is a well-recognised grand cru site.

Tasting note:
Characterised by medium body and lively acidity, 100% Marzemino wines have a red fruit dominant profile with hints of dried sage, almond, and a slightly bitter finish.

28. Montepulciano 🍇

One of Italy's most planted grapes, it accounts for half of the plantings in Abruzzo and is equally important to its neighbouring region, Marche. It must never be mistaken with Tuscany's Vino Nobile di Montepulciano DOCG which is based on Sangiovese. The most important wines made with Montepulciano include: Montepulciano d'Abruzzo DOC, Cerasuolo d'Abruzzo DOC; in Abruzzo: Abruzzo DOC and Rosso Piceno DOC and then Offida DOCG Rosso, Rosso Cònero DOC and Cònero DOCG in Marche. It can also be blended in the Molise DOC of Biferno Rosso. It also features as a blending grape in DOCs in Lazio and Puglia. Growing Montepulciano grapes can be a challenge as it requires more time to fully ripen.

Tasting note
In the glass, the wine sports a deep ruby, or purple hue. It is characterised by ripe cherry, plum, and delicate herb

nuances. Despite being typically full-bodied, it is not generally complex or age worthy beyond ten years. Styles can range from sparking, dry, sweet air-dried and rosatos. Rosatos can be pale pink to light ruby, and those labelled with Cerasuolo tend to be fleshier and more tannic with great complexity. Most often, it is cheerful, light, easy-going to rich, massive, with flavours of fleshy fruit with thick tannins.

29. Nascetta

The only white grape truly native to the Langhe, Nascetta was long confined exclusively to the hamlet of Novello, better known for Barolo production. Also called Anascetta or Nascëttà. After years of being overlooked, it was championed by wineries Elvio Cogno and Le Strette. Today, a growing number of producers are working to revive this grape. The wines labelled Anascetta del Comune di Novello are the original, or classic expressions and DOCs include Langhe DOC Nascetta, Langhe DOC Nascëtta del Comune di Novello.

Tasting note

Nascetta produces semi-aromatic wines. Youthful examples have herbal pungency reminiscent of Sauvignon Blanc and a balsamic minty character similar to Vermentino. It can also express orange, ginger, star fruit, sage and rosemary. A very saline edge gives it a savoury quality and an impression that the moderate acidity is higher than it actually is. Nascetta seems to age well, developing honey and vanilla notes.

30. Nebbiolo

Considered to be one of Italy's greatest native grapes. Theories suggest it is named according to the Latin word *Nebbia* (fog) since it is harvested during the time when fog is present in the vineyard or due to the heavy bloom of its grapes that remind one of fog. Nebbiolo's best known synonyms are Spanna (around Novara and Vercelli in Piedmont), Picotener (Valle d'Aosta) and Chiavennasca (Lombardy). Cultivated in northern Italian regions, the Nebbiolo present in Piedmont is used for Barolo DOCG, Barbaresco DOCG, Langhe DOC, Roero DOCG, Gattinara DOCG, Ghemme DOCG, and Carema DOC; in Lombardy for Rosso di Valtellina DOC, Valtellina Superiore DOCG, Sfursat di Valtellina DOCG; in Valle d'Aosta for Valle d'Aosta DOC Donnas.

Tasting note

Medium colour intensity with a garnet hue, even in youth. Nebbiolo is naturally high in tannins and acidity, making it age-worthy. Though some may think of Nebbiolo as giving aggressively tannic, tough wines, in reality, the best examples should be perfumed, exuding notes of red rose, sour red cherry and sweet spices. The aroma of tar develops with bottle age.

31. Negro Amaro

Although there are small plantings in Basilicata and Campania, the majority of Negro Amaro is found in Puglia, particularly in the Salice Salentino DOC. Don't be fooled, the amaro part of the name does not refer to a bitter, tannic aspect of the variety, rather the word amaro comes from the Greek, *mavros*, meaning black, referring to the dark colour of the berries. As a vine that can withstand heat whilst maintaining acidity, it is a variety increasingly looked to in times of climate change, not only in Italy, but around the world.

Tasting note

As suggested by "amaro" the hallmarks of this variety recall black notes: dark blue-black hues; black berries; black plums; black liquorice. However, it can be found in all styles, including wonderfully refreshing rosado thanks to its high acidity.

32. Nerello Cappuccio 🍇

Much rarer than its blending partner Nerello Mascalese, this vine gets its name from the bushy canopy that is said to resemble a cowl or cap (*cappuccio*) hiding the grapes from view. Rarely found on its own, the best expressions are the blends from the Etna Rosso DOC and Faro DOC.

Tasting note

With a deep dark red colour, Nerello Cappuccio provides colour to Nerello Mascalese and softens its acidity. It also gives fragrant red cherry, vanilla and mineral notes with subtle hints of coffee.

33. Nerello Mascalese 🍇

As Etna is now one of the most talked-about wine producing zones in the world, Nerello Mascalese is becoming a household name, and rightly so, given its propensity for exceptional complex and age-worthy wines, with many of the great Etna Rosso DOC wines being talked about in the same way as red Burgundy.

Tasting note

Nerello Mascalese is light in colour and has a great ability to translate terroir, resulting in subtle nuances between wines and vintages. Underlying all of this are pure aromas and flavours of sour cherry, tobacco, aromatic herbs and minerals.

Tannins can be green and astringent, so a short maceration and lower fermentation temperature is best, as is blending with the Nerello Cappuccio, a wine with lower tannins.

34. Nero d'Avola 🍇

Nero d'Avola is the modern, better-known name for the grape that locals often refer to as Calabrese. It has adapted well to Sicily's various terroirs over the centuries and can be found as incredibly expressive wines, helped by its ability to cope with salty soils and maintain acidity even in very warm conditions. Keep your eyes out for the wines of Pacino, a grand cru area that can present delicious savoury tomato leaf aromas.

Tasting Note

In recent times Nero d'Avola wines have been seen as a jack-of-all-trades, with many varying styles available. Those true to the variety have aromas of black plums and dark red cherry, bright acidity and a saline streak, others are marked by the use of new oak. Its classic blending partner is Frappato in the production of Cerasuolo di Vittoria DOCG.

35. Nosiola 🍇

Nosiola has been linked to Trentino since the 15th century and its isolated geographic location in small mountain-top vineyards saved it from being uprooted in favour of international varieties. Though various theories exist, most experts believe the name comes from nocciola, meaning hazelnut, due to the colour of the grapes and stalks when ripe, as well as the aromas of hazelnut the wine demonstrates. Sweet examples are made from late-harvested and air-dried grapes. Called Trentino Vino

Grapes or Places

It's not always obvious when looking at a wine label what refers to what, and as a result, you might find yourself in a wine shop or a restaurant playing one of our favourite games, grape or place! We thought it might be useful to have a diagram to make it simpler.

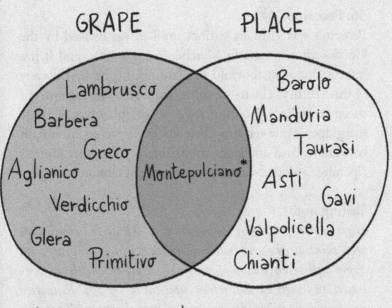

* We said "simple" not easy!

Santo, these are unctuously sweet, rich and complex, with ripe peach, almond paste, lime, candied pineapple, tropical fruit jelly aromas and flavours.

36. Pecorino

Pecorino was virtually extinct until it was revived by the Cocci Grifoni estate in Marche, in the 1980s, and it has increased almost fourfold in plantings in the first decade of this century. The name comes from *pecora*, which means sheep in Italian. Pecorino refers to sheepherders who ate the grapes while tending their flocks. It prefers mountain conditions and manages to maintain its acidity during ripening, a vital characteristic in times of climate change.

37. Picolit

With a noble past, Picolit is a Friulian white grape, capable of giving world-class sweet wine. Picolit is one of the most ancient Italian native grapes. Colli Orientali del Friuli Picolit DOCG is a sweet wine, ranging from off-dry to lusciously sweet. Nowadays it is mostly made with the appassimento method, but some producers are scaling back from making overly jammy thick wines that lose Picolit's wonderful delicacy and refinement. Picolit is also used in blends to give texture and sweetness. It can be also found in the Collio DOC and Friuli Colli Orientali DOC.

Tasting note

Usually made into a sweet wine. Bright yellow to amber-gold in colour, Picolit wine tastes delicately of acacia honey, dried mango, pineapple, candied ginger and nectarine. Its graceful and refined texture is what makes Picolit sweet wine exceptional. However, it does not seem to develop more complex notes with time so is not considered particularly age-worthy.

38. Prié

Better known as Prié Blanc, this Valle d'Aosta native grape grows in some of the highest vineyards in Europe. Its name refers to its usage in Sunday Mass (*prier* means to pray in French). Prié is the oldest documented grape in Valle d'Aosta. Still, dry whites are the most typical, yet sparkling and sweet wines of Prié Blanc are also made. Planted in Valle d'Aosta, the most notable wine is that of the subzone Blanc de Morgex et de La Salle.

Tasting note

Delicately floral, steely and with bright acidity, the Blanc de Morgex et La Salle wines are made from 100% Prié and is one of Italy's best light-bodied white wines, making it an ideal apéritif.

39. Refosco dal Peduncolo Rosso 🍇

The most famous and important of Refoscos and likely Friuli-Venezia Giulia's best-known red grape. Peduncolo Rosso translates as 'red stalk' as indeed its stalks turn red when fully ripe. Used to produce still red wines in Friuli-Venezia Giulia can be found in Friuli Colli Orientali DOC, Friuli Grave DOC.

Tasting note

The most aromatically complex of the Refoscos, it demonstrates dried red cherry, fresh herbs, almonds and floral nuances of lavender, geranium and violet. However, these notes often fail to linger. Small barrels are frequently used for ageing in order to help smooth Refosco dal Peduncolo Rosso's tannins, which can be tough and astringent and curbs reduction, which this grape has a tendency towards. Similar to the Cabernets, it can show green notes, especially when not fully ripe.

40. Ribolla Gialla 🍇

A high-quality white variety with a long history of production and export. Numerous spelling variants such as Ràbola, Rebolla, and Ribuèle. Usually dry, light, and fresh, but also commonly used to make 'orange wines' using extended skin contact and oxidative techniques. Some producers are testing its suitability – because of its high acidity – for sparkling wine, but with mixed results. Despite all the media buzz surrounding these new Ribollas, the best Ribolla Gialla wines are still those made from low cropping old vines, on hilltop vineyards that give classically dry, perfumed white wines. Friuli Colli Orientali DOC and Collio DOC are the main DOCs.

41. Rondinella

This is a variety that has been more successful post-phylloxera and seems to have improved by being grafted onto American rootstocks. Its name comes from rondine, meaning swallow; either Rondinella's dark colour recalls this bird's plumage, or quite simply these small birds like to feed on Rondinella when it is ripe. It is primarily used as a supporting grape in the Veneto wines of the Valpolicella DOC, Valpolicella Ripasso DOC, Amarone della Valpolicella DOCG, Recioto della Valpolicella DOCG, Bardolino DOC and Bardolino Superiore DOCG.

42. Rossese

Cultivation of Rossese is limited to a small section of western Liguria where vines cling to steep mountain-sides above the Ligurian sea. Think rosso, which refers to the berries' red colouration. There are several genetically distinct Rossese. The most famous is Rossese di Dolceacqua, which is better quality and more widely cultivated. Though both made from Rossese, Riviera Ligure di Ponente DOC wines are neutral, lightly fruity and thin compared to those of Rossese di Dolceacqua DOC which are more intense, salty and spicy with greater depth of fruit.

Tasting note
Bright, clear ruby red hue. It offers pretty fragrances of violets, redcurrants, graphite, roses and sometimes strawberries. The finest wines have a salty-sour component of red currant and cranberry. With vibrant acid and a dry mouthfeel, Rossese is graceful and charming; best drunk within 2 years of the vintage, though some can age a remarkable 8-10 years.

43. Ruché

An excellent example of one of the few aromatic red grape varieties in Italy. Its name may be a reference to roncet, a viral disease that Ruché is less susceptible to than are most Piemontese varieties. Its DOC is Ruchè di Castagnole Monferrato DOCG.

Tasting note
The aromatic nature of the variety is expressed as flowers such as rose, lavender and iris as well as spices like black pepper, mint, coriander, cinnamon and nutmeg.

44. Sagrantino

Theory exists that the name possibly comes from *sacrestia*, a church room where a priest prepares for mass as this wine is traditionally served for during religious services. It was first notable for sweet, passito style wine in the first

DOC in 1977. Nowadays, dry still wines dominate in the Umbrian denominations of Sagrantino di Montefalco DOCG and Montefalco DOC.

Tasting note

This is a wine dark in colour, but with tannins that are sleek and polished. The wines are very long-lived and the best examples are complex with a mélange of wild, dark berries, dried plums, cocoa, tar, tobacco, cinnamon, dried herbs and balsamic notes. The DOCG wines of Sagrantino di Montefalco are monovarietal and can be dry or sweet passito styles. Sagrantino is often used as a blend with Sangiovese to add weight, colour and tannin as done in DOC Montefalco.

45. Sangiovese 🍇

The number one most-planted grape variety in Italy. It's etymology and its origin are simply not agreed upon by experts. Sangiovese's proliferation has led to numerous names in different zones: Morellino in Scansano on the Tuscan coast, Brunello in Montalcino, Prugnolo Gentile in Montepulciano, and Sangiovese di Lamole and Sangioveto in parts of Chianti Classico. The key Sangiovese based DOCs are Chianti DOCG, Chianti Classico DOCG, Rosso di Montalcino DOC, Brunello di Montalcino DOCG, Rosso di Montepulciano DOC, Vino Nobile di Montepulciano DOCG, Morellino di Scansano DOCG; Carmignano DOCG in Tuscany; Rosso Piceno DOC in Marche and Romagna DOC in Emilia Romagna.

Tasting note

Ranging from brilliant ruby to garnet, true Sangiovese wines should never be jet black in colour because of the variety's anthocyanin composition. Overall, Sangiovese shows aromas of red and black cherry, liquorice, black tea and nuances of violet. With age, leather, undergrowth and even tobacco start to emerge. Regardless, Sangiovese always has high acidity and pronounced chalky tannins.

46. Schiava Gentile 🍇

Also known as Schiava Piccola due to its small (though sometime medium-sized) bunches. Late ripening, low yields and small berries give it a reputation for producing quality juice.

Tasting note

Schiava Gentile produces reds that are dark pink to pale ruby in hue with fresh red fruit (red currant, sour red cherry, strawberry) and floral notes (buttercup and violets). The rosato is prized thanks to its perfumed aromas, light body and high acid.

47. Schioppettino 🍇

Virtually extinct by the 1970's, Schioppettino was revived in large part by the Rapuzzi family, owners of the Ronchi di Cialla estate; vital in getting this grape recognised by the DOC. The word *scoppiettare* means "to explode", so the grape's name may refer to an explosion of flavour or a propensity for the wine to referment and explode in the bottle in earlier days. It is primarily used in Friuli Colli Orientali DOC, especially in the Cialla and Prepotto subzones.

Tasting note

A dry, still, medium-bodied red, high in acid, with aromas and flavours of blackcurrant, black cherry, and characteristic green peppercorn. With age these wines may develop underbrush and tar notes.

48. Teroldego 🍇

Trentino's signature red grape. It is found to be a parent of Lagrein and Marzemino. Used mostly for Trentino DOC, Teroldego Rotaliano DOC and IGP Vigneti delle Dolomiti wines. A well-recognised quality site is Campo Rotaliano. While most of its plantings are found in Trentino, it is also cultivated in Tuscany and Sicily.

Tasting note

Famed for its deep colour, Teroldego wines show bright fruit and supple tannins, featuring aromas and flavours such as red and black cherry, tar, fresh spices and herbs. A vegetal streak is noticeable when it is under ripe and therefore, picking times are key.

49. Timorasso 🍇

Once Piedmont's most commonly grown white (along with Cortese) it was almost abandoned due to viticultural challenges. Walter Massa is credited with resurrecting Timorasso starting in the eighties, and today there are over thirty producers. It is regarded as one of Italy's exciting up and coming whites, but despite the hype, the proof is not always in the glass. Used mainly in Colli Tortonesi DOC.

50. Tintilia

The key red grape of Molise, some experts believed it was brought there from Spain. The name (*Tintiglia* or *Tintilia*) could easily derive from the Spanish *tinto*, meaning red, however in Italian, calling something tinto also means that it is coloured. Whilst it was traditionally used as a blending grape, it is now holding its own in the wines of the DOC Tintilia del Molise.

Tasting note

Pleasantly spicy and floral on the nose, it is full-bodied, with flavours of ripe red fruit, leather, and tobacco, mineral notes of flint and tar and a pleasant saline bent, with very good acidity and noble tannins.

51. Primitivo

One of Italy's top ten planted red grape varieties, its popularity keeps growing. Its name comes from its early ripening habit. Indeed, it is often the first grape to be picked in Italy, with harvests beginning as early as August. Whilst it ripens unevenly (meaning some grapes become raisins whilst others remain green) it also accumulates sugar easily – not an easy grape to decide when to pick! Perhaps the most famous wines are those of Primitivo di Manduria DOC.

Tasting note

Deeply coloured wines that tend to lose their colour quickly as they age. Primitivo wines typically have appealing aromas of ripe red cherry, strawberry jam and plums macerated in alcohol which carry through on the creamy rich palate. High heady alcohol, upwards of 16% is common, although well integrated with the power of the aromas and flavours, and often balanced by a pleasant herbal finish.

52. Verdicchio

This noble Italian grape is capable of giving highly age-worthy wine. Named after the colour green, *verde,* this grape is mostly associated with the Marche and the Veneto. Famous wines are Verdicchio dei Castelli di Jesi DOC (and Riserva DOCG) and Verdicchio di Matelica DOC (and Riserva DOCG), from the Marche and Lugana DOC from the Veneto. The grape can adapt to different sites. It ripens slowly while maintaining high acidity, which helps in age ability and complexity.

Tasting note

Pale, straw yellow with a green tinge in colour. Typical aromas and flavours are lemon zest, sweet almond and white flowers, supported by medium plus to high acid. When aged, it can develop a Riesling like flintiness. One of the few Italian whites that can age well in oak to enhance ageing and complexity.

53. Vermentino/Favorita/Pigato 🍇

Though officially listed as three separate varieties, Vermentino, Favorita, and Pigato are genetically a single variety. They are also known around the world by various synonyms. It should be noted that the wines from this grape in their home region are incredibly expressive and have adapted to the terroir perfectly, providing for very different wines and styles, hence why producers prefer to stick to their local name to maintain regional identity. As Vermentino, this variety is grown mainly in Sardinia, Tuscany, and Liguria. It is often called Favorita in Piedmont, and Pigato in western Liguria. Arguably one of the best examples is found in the Vermentino di Gallura DOCG.

Tasting note

As perhaps can be expected from its introduction, this variety has a wide range of aromas and flavours, including acacia flowers, rosemary, thyme, citrus, peach, apricot, apple, and tropical fruit. Some are said to have a saline finish, and those labelled Pigato can be richer and creamier, but still with the hallmark salinity.

54. Vernaccia 🍇

Vernaccia is a name given to a large collection of grapes scattered all over Italy. One of the most important is Vernaccia di San Gimignano. It takes its name from San Gimignano, a medieval hilltop located in Tuscany that was awarded the first DOC wine in Italy, that is now a DOCG.

Tasting note

The unoaked version of this wine is pale yellow in colour, sometimes with green tinges. Clean, fresh versions have lemon zest and sage, with hints of almond at the end. Most styles that can be found are still, dry white. Riserva versions may be oaked, with hints of vanilla and can be balanced. Exceptional examples of wines are found that utilise lees ageing to soften the acidity and give complexity and body.

55. Uva di Troia 🍇

Now the third most planted red in Puglia, Uva di Troia's enormous increase in monovarietal bottlings and blends are due to an overall renewed interest in Italy's native grapes. The term Nero di Troia is a new synonym, one that only started being used at the beginning of the 21st century already in common use but its official name is still Uva di Troia. Like Primitivo, it ripens unevenly, takes a long time to ripen completely and is subject to sunburn, however, its worth battling these issues as the result is quite delicious!

Tasting note

Uva di Troia offers nuances of red cherries, red currants, black pepper, tobacco and underbrush. It is medium in weight with high yet refined tannins and is often used to bring freshness and finesse to blends with Primitivo, Negro Amaro and Aglianico.

4. GREAT ITALIAN (GRAPE) FAMILIES

It's not just people that have families, some grapes do to! One of the things that can be confusing about Italian wine is the numerous grapes that share common or similar names, and whilst this can be a tricky topic when you really dive deep, (there are *how many* Malvasia?!), it is possible to make it much simpler. We've selected the most famous of these grapes and handily divided them up for you.

FAMILIES
These are grapes that not only share a name but are also related.

Moscato

Let's start with the hardest! Not all Moscato are related. However, most are and so we call them a family.
Moscato (or Muscat, in English) shows itself in a range of skin colours, from yellow to pink, to rosy red and even some which border on a deep garnet. A common thread shared by this family, and perhaps its most recognisable trait, is a distinct aromatic quality; aromas of orange blossom, pineapple, honey, sage and rose are typical of this sweet-smelling family.

KEY MEMBERS

Moscato Bianco: the most abundant of all the family members; Moscato Bianco has been shown through scientific studies to be the progenitor from which all other Moscato varieties have evolved. This is the grape from which the delicious Moscato d'Asti wine is made.
Moscato di Alessandria/Zibibbo: Moscato di Alessan-

dria, also called Zibibbo in Sicily, is the offspring of Moscato Bianco. Highly associated with the island of Pantelleria, Moscato di Alessandria makes profound dry and sweet style wines that are incredibly aromatic.

Lambrusco

The famous red grape used to make delicious sparkling wines in Emilia Romagna, the Lambrusco family is having a rightful comeback!

Mainly associated with Emilia Romagna, the Lambrusco clan is likely Italy's oldest family of native grapes. Typically made as sparkling reds and occasionally rosatos, these are mostly either dry (secco) or off-dry (semi-secco), but can sometimes be sweet (dolce). They are often floral and fragrant, delicious with cured meats.

KEY MEMBERS

Lambrusco di Sorbara: the oldest member of the Lambrusco family. It is also called Lambrusco della Viola due to the intense violet aromas of these pale pink delicately textured wines. It is often blended with Lambrusco Salamino.

Lambrusco Grasparossa: it is also knowns as Lambrusco di Castelvetro after its birthplace around the town of Castelvetro. This is the powerhouse of the Lambrusco family, rich deep purple in colour with delightfully intense aromas and flavours of black cherry and plum.

Lambrusco Salamino: Lambrusco Salamino is the most abundantly planted of all the Lambruscos. Its long (but small) cylindrical bunches are said to be reminiscent of a salame! It is often partnered with Lambrusco di Sorbara, making wines that are said to have the scents of the Sorbara variety, but with the power of Grasparossa – the best of both worlds!

Sparkling Wines in Italy

There's been a real buzz about the bubbles out of Italy in the last few years! As their popularity has increased, so have the number of bottles produced, and the international market has truly embraced these wines.

Whilst many people think Italian sparkling wine is synonymous with Prosecco, this is not actually the case. Italy is home to numerous types and styles, as sparkling wine is an important part of Italian wine life and culture. Fizz is found not only in light fruity white styles, but also in everything from aromatic, sweet and gently effervescent wine (from the Piemonte Asti DOCG), to refreshing rosés and reds (found in the various Lambrusco designations of Emilia Romagna), all the way to the richly complex, bold and biscuity wines (from the Franciacorta and Trento DOC).

The insatiable appetite for affordable sparkling wines, and the great suitability of many Italian grape varietals to this production method – high acidity, defined fruit character – means that there is even scope for other Italian regions to experiment and create new appealing wines with their native varieties. One of the most important examples of a new sparkling area, becoming more important day by day, is Alta Langa DOCG in Piedmont, we are even seeing the production of sparkling wines from Carricante in Sicily. Italian sparkling wines are made historically using one of three different techniques: the Traditional Method, the Tank Method or the Asti Method.

Traditional Method - Metodo Classico

The Traditional Method of sparkling winemaking is probably the most appreciated method for sparkling wine production in terms of quality because it creates complex and structured wines with characteristics beyond the grape variety itself. The most important facet of the traditional method is that the transformation from a still to a sparkling wine occurs entirely inside the bottle.

The Traditional Method could be described in the following way: a low alcohol dry "base" wine is made. The winemaker then takes various base wines, from different grape varieties or even different vintages, and blends them together. To this existing wine they then add what is called *Liquer de Tirage*, a mixture of yeast and sugars that start the second fermentation that take place in the bottle. This second fermentation adds about 1.3% more alcohol, and the process creates CO_2 gas which is trapped inside the bottle, thus carbonating the wine. The yeast dies in a process called autolysis and it remains in the bottle. These dead yeast cells form a sediment called lees and it is from being left on these that Metodo Classico wines gain their texture, complexity and much of their flavour.

When the winemaker is ready to remove the lees from the wines they will slowly begin turning the bottle so that the dead yeast cells collect in the neck. As soon as all the yeast is here they will remove the sediment in a process called *disgorging*: the bottles are placed upside down into freezing liquid which causes the yeast bits to freeze in the neck of the bottle. The temporary cap is then popped off momentarily which allows the frozen chunk of lees to shoot out of the pressurized bottle. In order for the bottle to be full when purchased and at the right level of sweetness, a *dosage* of wine and sugar (called exposition liqueur) is added. Now the bottles are ready to be corked, wired and labelled.

Traditional Method is typical for Franciacorta DOCG, Oltrepò Pavese Metodo Calssico DOCG, Trento DOC and Alta Langa DOCG and gives wines with complex biscuity, yeasty, doughy aromas, in addition to those such as ripe apple, lemon or other fruit flavours from the grape variety. These are also wines that often benefit from further ageing in the bottle.

Tank Method - Charmat Method, Metodo Martinotti

The key difference between Tank Method and Traditional Method sparkling wines is where the second fermentation takes place. Rather than relying on this to happen in individual bottles, in the Tank Method, base wines are added together with the sugar and yeast mixture into, you guessed it, a large tank!

As the wine still undergoes a second fermentation, the CO_2 released from the fermentation causes the tank to pressurise, once complete, the wines are then filtered, dosed and bottled without ageing.

Tank Method sparkling wines have a much more freshly made character with stronger fruit and flower flavours, they are ideally suited for making wines using aromatic grape varieties. While the process is more affordable than the Metodo Classico, it is still used for fine sparkling winemaking and should not be considered a "lesser" style, simply a different style. Tank Method is typical for the Lambrusco DOCs, Prosecco DOC and Prosecco DOCG, all of which are wines that express clear fruit characteristics, whether these are the fresh red cherry and plum from Lambrusco, or the white peach and blossom of Glera in Prosecco.

Asti Method

This method is principally used for the production of sweet sparkling wines in the Asti region of Piedmont which is why the name has stuck. It produces sweet fruity sparkling wines but is somewhat unusual in that unlike the other methods it relies on only one alcoholic fermentation. The pressed grape juice is chilled and stored until needed, then, when it is required, it is gently warmed up so that fermentation takes place in pressurised tanks. The fermentation continues until the alcohol has reached around 5-5.5%, and a light sparkle has been achieved. The fermentation is stopped early by chilling the wine, which is then filtered under pressure and bottled.

Asti Method is mainly used in for the Asti DOCG using Moscato Bianco grapes. These are incredibly intense and aromatic wines, with clear grape, peach and white flower aromas and flavours. Don't be scared of their sweetness, they are exceptional wines and perfect for aperitivos or even with Pannetone at breakfast on a festive occasion!

Grape Varieties in Italian sparkling

Whilst in Italy there are a huge amount of native grape varieties being used for sparkling wines, the focus has remained - particularly for the Traditional Method wines on the international varieties found in so many of these wines around the world. The most commonnly found are Chardonnay, Pinot Nero (Pinot Noir) and Pinot Bianco.

91

GROUPS

These grapes share a name but are not related! Instead they have gained their moniker from historical or cultural events.

Malvasia

Perhaps the most confusing and extensive group of grapes in Italy, with more than 17 members, they seem to be everywhere!

The fact that at least seventeen grapes sport the Malvasia moniker in Italy hints at Malvalsia's once unbeatable fame. In fact, Malvasia was the best-known wine from the fourteenth to the seventeenth century thanks to the seafaring Venetians, who dominated the Mediterranean Sea and traded Malvasia wine with tremendous success. They were Italy's first brand name, before "Italy" even existed!

KEY MEMBERS

Malvasia Istriana White: produces some of the best dry white Malvasia wines in Italy. As its name implies, it is thought to have originated from Croatia's Istrian peninsula, which belonged to Italy before WWII. Studies show that it is genetically related to Malvasia di Lipari and Malvasia Bianca Lunga. Mostly found in Friuli-Venezia Giulia with marginal plantings in Puglia and Veneto. Main DOC are Carso DOC, Collio DOC and Friuli Isonzo DOC. Usually it gives still dry white wine. Some macerated examples show a fuller body and a more impressive tannic structure.

Its wine shows a pale colour except if macerated for long periods. Some examples demonstrate a softly aromatic character which may be attributed to lower yields, doing a pre-fermentation cold soak. Its style ranges from mineral and austere, to full-bodied and alcoholic depending on specific sites. The best are delicately floral and remarkably saline. With time, it develops notes of apricot, peach and wisteria and even a Riesling-like diesel note.

Malvasia di Candia Aromatica White: producing wines that have mildly aromatic notes of tropical fruits and spices, Malvasia di Candia Aromatica is typical of the Emilia part of Emilia Romagna. There it makes varietal wine. It is also found in Lazio as well as Lombardy where it shows up in blends of Oltrepò Pavese. Note that Malvasia di Candia Aromatica is completely different from Malvasia Bianca di Candia, which is a non-aromatic variety and generally considered to be of a lower quality.

Greco

A small but mighty group that is important as they are often confused with not only each other, but where they come from.

Although it possesses a short, sweet name, understanding the Greco group can be somewhat challenging. It does not in fact refer to the wines being from "Greece" but instead is another brand name given to wines made in the "Greek style" which tagged onto the popularity started by the interest in Malvasia!

KEY MEMBERS

Greco: The easiest Greco to remember, is... Greco! But equally important to remember is that Greco is the name of the grape variety; Greco di Tufo is the name of the denomination in Campania that produces wine using the Greco variety. The name of the variety is simply Greco; calling the variety Greco di Tufo is incorrect, yet a common mistake.

A truly great white grape of Italy, Greco's wines show depth

Wines to discover

In recent years many producers across Italy's regions have started to rediscover ancient local native grapes varieties. They have started to focus on them, identifying the right soils and growing conditions, in combination with the best winemaking techniques. Some of these have already arrived in the international market, but others, whilst less known, are suddenly receiving the recognition they deserve. Here is a selection that we think you should hunt out, try and enjoy, so that we can all support the produers who are so gallantly saving or pushing them!

WINE FORECAST

Nerello Mascalese   Pecorino

Erbamat   Grignolino

Timorasso   Granaccia

Pigato   Alta Langa

Bombino Nero   Ruché

and impressive structure, a nice golden yellow hue, high alcohol, a rich palate, an unmistakable oily mouthfeel, yet with marked acidity. Aromas run the gamut from flowers to peaches and honey. Best of all, the wines drink well when young and have the potential for great ageing. In fact, as soon as you put this book down go and find one!

Greco Bianco White: Here we go again with the confusing life of the Greco group! Greco Bianco is the name of a grape variety, but Greco di Bianco is the name of a DOC in Calabria responsible for making ripe, honeyed, air-dried wines from the Greco Bianco grape.

Trebbiano

A group that share not only their name, but also many character traits!

Trebbianos group members are characterised by high vigour and yield, long and large bunches, late-ripening and are very adaptive to different terroirs. This explains why over the centuries these altogether different varieties have been lumped together and named together.

KEY MEMBERS

Trebbiano Abruzzese: here we go again! – the correct name of this grape is Trebbiano Abruzzese, while Trebbiano d'Abruzzo is the name of its wine. Unlike most other Trebbianos, the grapes of Trebbiano Abruzzese remain deep straw green even when ripe. Pale straw lemon in colour, wines of Trebbiano Abruzzese exude scents of lemon and peach with a hint of white flower. The dense texture noted. on the palate is supported by bright acidity and mineral savouriness, reductive winemaking with this variety is gaining currency. The drawback with this is that the wines resemble Sauvignon Blanc rather than expressing the true characteristics of Trebbiano Abruzzese.

Trebbiano Toscano: the most widely planted white variety in Italy and also found across the border in France where it is known as Ugni Blanc. Undeniably Italian, one fun fact about this variety is that it was used to create Vidal, one of the most commercially successfully hybrids, famous for its role in the production of many Canadian ice wines.

5. WHY ITALIANS DO IT BETTER

A CULINARY JOURNEY THROUGH ITALY

It is no doubt that wine and food always come together. Just like wine, every region in Italy is also characterised by its cuisine. If there are more than 600 grapes varieties, maybe there are even more traditional recipes, in fact, not only does every region have its own traditional dishes, but sometimes culinary traditions are different from town to town. Regional cuisine in Italy is extremely diverse, and a source of pride for Italians! Here, we propose a little journey through Italy to discover some of the most representative food, it wasn't easy, but we chose our favourites; dishes or recipes that you might come across.

We also included a little tip for a wine pairing if you are travelling and eating in the most important Italian cities, based on our experience. We deliberately left the names of the food in their original Italian or dialect so that you will sound like a native when ordering! Buon appetito and cin cin!

1. Valle d'Aosta
- Main food: *Fontina Valdostana DOP, Lardo di Arnad DOP, Fonduta, Cotoletta Valdostana*
- Main City: Aosta
- If you are travelling here, you have to try *Fonduta with Val d'Aosta Torrette DOC*

2. Piedmont
- Main food: *Agnolotti del Plin, Tartufo Bianco di Alba, Brasato al Barolo, Carne all'Albese, Bollito misto Piemontese, Fritto Misto Piemontese, Tajarin al tartufo, Bagna Caoda*

🏛 Main City: Turin

🥂 If you are travelling here, you have to try
Bollito Misto Piemontese with Barolo DOCG

3. Liguria

🍖 Main food: *Pesto, Verdure ripiene, Coniglia alla ligure,*
Cappon Magro, Focaccia Genovese, Farinata,
Bagnun di Acciughe

🏛 Main City: Genova

🥂 If you are travelling here, you have to try *Trenette al*
Pesto with Pigato Riviera Ligure di Ponente DOC

4. Lombardy

🍖 Main food: *Risotto alla Milanese, Pizzoccheri*
della Valtellina, Gorgonzola DOP, Cassoeula,
Ossobusco alla Milanese, Bresaola della Valtellina DOP,
Grana Padano DOP

🏛 Main City: Milan

🥂 If you are travelling here, you have to try *Risotto*
alla Milanese with Franciacorta Saten DOCG

5. Veneto

🍖 Main food: *Asiago DOP, Monte Veronese DOP,*
Baccalà alla Vicentina, Sarde in Saor, Bigoli,
Tiramisù, Cicheti, Soppressa Veneta, Radiccio
Trevigiano DOP

🏛 Main City: Venice

🥂 If you are travelling here, you have to try
Cicheti with Prosecco di Conegliano
Valdobbiadene DOCG

Northern Italy   Central Italy   Southern Italy
& the Islands

6. Trentino-Alto Adige

🍖 Main food: *Speck DOP, Canederli, Spatzle, Polenta, Tortei di Patate, Strudel*

🏛 Main City: Trento

🍴 If you are travelling here, you have to try *Canederli allo Speck with Teroldego Rotaliano DOC*

7. Friuli-Venezia Giulia

🍖 Main food: *Prosciutto di San Daniele DOP, Frico, Prosciutto di Sauris, Cjarsons*

🏛 Main City: Trieste

🍴 If you are travelling here, you have to try *Frico with Friulano Collio DOC*

8. Emilia Romagna

🍖 Main food: P*armigiano Reggiano DOP, Prosciutto di Parma DOP, Tortellini, Lasagne alla Bolognese, Mortadella, Piadina Romagnola, Tigelle*

🏛 Main City: Bologna

🍴 If you are travelling here, you have to try *Lasagne alla Bolognese with Sangiovese di Romagna DOC*

9. Tuscany

🍖 Main food: *Bistecca alla Fiorentina, Caciucco alla Livornese, Ribollita, Pappa al pomodoro, Pecorino Toscano, Pappardelle al Cinghiale, Panzanella, Lardo di Colonnata, Prosciutto Toscano*

🏛 Main City: Florence

🍴 If you are travelling here, you have to try *Bistecca alla Fiorentina with Chianti Classico DOCG*

10. Umbria

● Main food: *Strangozzi al Tartufo nero, Prosciutto Crudo di Norcia, Salami, Torta al Testo*

🏛 Main City: Perugia

🍴 If you are travelling here, you have to try *Strangozzi al Tartufo Nero with Montefalco Rosso DOC*

11. Marche

● Main food: *Olive all'Ascolana, Ciauscolo, Crescia, Brodetto*

🏛 Main City: Ancona

🍴 If you are travelling here, you have to try *Brodetto with Verdicchio di Jesi DOC*

12. Lazio

● Main food: *Pecorino Romano, Bucatini all'Amatriciana, Carbonara, Cacio e Pepe, Porchetta di Ariccia, Coratella, Carciofi alla Giudia, Saltimbocca alla Romana, Trippe*

🏛 Main City: Rome

🍴 If you are travelling here, you have to try *Bucatini all'Amatriciana with Cesanese del Piglio DOCG*

13. Abruzzo

● Main food: *Arrosticini, Sagne e Fagioli, Pasta con gli Scampi, Cozze allo Zafferano dell'Aquila, Crudo di Calamaretti, Scapece, Pallotte Caci e Ova*

🏛 Main City: L'Aquila

🍴 If you are travelling here, you have to try *Arrosticini with Montepulciano d'Abruzzo DOC*

14. Molise

🍲 Main food: *Ventricina di Montenero di Bisaccia, Soppressata del Molise, Scamorza Molisana, tartufo Molisano*

🏛 Main City: Campobasso

🍴 If you are travelling here, you have to try *Maccheroni al Tartufo with Tintilia del Molise DOC*

15. Campania

🍲 Main food: *Pizza Napoletana, Mozzarela di Bufala Campana, Casatiello, Impepata di Cozze, Friarielli, Babà, Pastiera Napoletana, Sfogliatelle*

🏛 Main City: Naples

🍴 If you are travelling here, you have to try *Pizza Margherita with Fiano di Avellino DOC*

16. Puglia

🍲 Main food: *Orecchiette con le Cime di Rapa, Burrata, Tiella di Riso Patate e Cozze, Bombette pugliesi, Focaccia Barese, Pasticciotto*

🏛 Main City: Bari

🍴 If you are travelling here, you have to try *Tiella di Riso Patate e Cozze with Salice Salentino Rosato DOC*

17. Basilicata

🍲 Main food: *Caciocavallo Podolico, Peperoni Cruschi, Salsiccia Lucanica, Ragù Lucano, Cicoria e Fave, Bollito dei Pastori*

🏛 Main City: Potenza

🍴 If you are travelling here, you have to try *Ragù Lucano with Aglianco del Vulture DOC*

18. Calabria

- 🐗 Main food: *Peperoncino di Soverato, Cipolla di Tropea, Spianata Piccante, 'Nduja, Maccaruni aru Fierru, Purpetti*
- 🏛 Main City: Catanzaro
- 🍴 If you are travelling here, you have to try *Maccaruni aru Fierru with Cirò Rosso DOC*

19. Sicily

- 🐗 Main food: *Pasta alla Norma, Pasta con le Sarde, Cous Cous di Pesce, Panelle, Arancini di Riso, Sarde a Beccafico, Cannolo di Ricotta, Cassata, Granita Siciliana*
- 🏛 Main City: Palermo
- 🍴 If you are travelling here, you have to try *Cassata Siciliana with Passito di Pantelleria DOC*

20. Sardinia

- 🐗 Main food: *Pecorino Sardo DOP, Fregola con Frutti di Mare e Zafferano, Spaghetti con i Ricci di Mare, Porcheddu, Bottarga, Seadas*
- 🏛 Main City: Cagliari
- 🍴 If you are travelling here, you have to try *Fregola con Frutti di Mare e Zafferano with Vermentino di Gallura Rosato DOCG*

FUN FAQS

We reached out to our friends and colleagues working in wine retail and hospitality sector to see what questions they most commonly faced when selling Italian wine, this is what they told us, and these were the answers we gave to help them and their customers.

"What is a *Supertuscan*, and what makes it super?"

Supertuscan wines are those from a particular area of Tuscany near Bolgheri that have historically focused on making wines using so-called international varieties such as Merlot, Cabernet Sauvignon, and Cabernet Franc, rather than Sangiovese. These wines were designed to provide a native answer to the popular and expensive wines from Bordeaux. As they fell outside of the local DOC and DOCG guidelines they could only be labelled as IGT or Vino da Tavola, and yet their quality and popularity meant they commanded prices that were often much higher than their DOC counterparts. Hence, they became known as "Supertuscans". Some of these wines have now been granted DOC recognition, but their original name has stuck and so they will forever be the super wines of Tuscany.

"Why does this Prosecco say it's Extra Dry but is actually sweeter than the other one?"

As if Italian names and labels weren't already confusing enough, let's consider their labelling of sweetness levels for sparkling wines! Probably the most useful thing to understand is that the Italians label truly "dry" wines (those with less than 6g of residual sugar per litre) as "Brut". This is what you're looking for if you like dry wine. Wines labelled as "Extra Brut" are actually those with a little bit of sugar retained during the fermentation. They are not truly sweet wines but tend to have a softer texture and hint of sweetness, perhaps even more ripeness of fruit flavours. Whilst many people avoid these styles fearing they will be sickly and not enjoyable, we urge you to try them. They are utterly delicious aperitivo wines.

"Why is this white wine called orange?"

Orange wines are wines made from white grape varieties, but with "red winemaking" techniques. The alcoholic fermentation occurs with full skin contact, and this concentrates the colour, making it more orange than yellow. Often these wines also experience oxidative ageing in containers like amphoras (large clay pots) and this accentuates the orange hint. Even if the words "orange wine" are internationally used, it is more correct to call these wines "skin contact fermented white wine". In Italy you can find these wines all over the peninsula, but they are more "traditional" in the north east area, Friuli-Venezia Giulia in particular.

"Is this Cerasuolo a rosé or a red wine?"

Well, the truth is it could be both! "Cerasuolo" is a term that comes from "cherry" in Italian and is used for both red and rosé wines. However, there are two wines that "officially" take this name. The first is Cerasuolo d'Abruzzo. This is a rosé wine made from Montepulciano grapes in the region of Abruzzo. They can be deeply coloured but dry wines with bright red berry flavours and a gentle texture. The other is "Cerasuolo di Vittoria" these are red wines from Sicily, made with a blend of Frappato and Nero d'Avola grapes, they can both have a clear strawberry aroma and a lovely savoury tomato leaf character also Another aspect they share is that they are both of course equally delicious!

"Is Prosecco and Cava made in the same way?"
No, they aren't. Cava is made with the traditional method, so the second fermentation takes place in the bottle. Prosecco is traditionally made with the Tank Method (Martinotti or Charmat) and are characterised by intense primary and secondary fruit aromas, typical for this method. Cava is usually made with a shorter mat-

– What's the best wine to improve my Italian fluency?

uration period in the bottle, so the yeasty and ageing aromas you might expect don't have time to develop. While Cava is more floral and citrusy, Prosecco is more fruity, with typical apple and pear aromas, particularly intense in the traditional area of Conegliano and Valdobbiadene DOCG. There are some Prosecco, called Col Fondo, which see some lees ageing in the bottle, and indeed some that are made in the Metodo Classico style, but they are not very common as it's the fruity aromatic character that most producers believe show off this style best. We'll let you decide!

And finally, the question everyone asks but no one can truly answer...

"How do I match an Italian wine to food?"

That's a tricky one, and even the Italians disagree about this all the time! But a good rule of thumb is to think about the cuisine of the region where the wine came from. For example, Lambrusco from Emilia Romagna is a great choice for the mortadella or tortellini that are synonymous with the region. Nero d'Avola is lovely when enjoyed with tomato dishes as there are many of these found in the area of Sicily near Pachino where the famous cherry tomatoes are grown. Vermentino often finds its home growing near the sea and so can be a nice choice for seafood dishes. But, there really is no right answers to this question, we recommend that you simply enjoy your wine with good food and good company!

If you like... then try

There's almost always an Italian alternative to your usual or favourite wine!

Cava?
Prosecco Valdobbiadene o Alta Langa

Marlborough Sauvignon Blanc?
Collio Sauvignon

White Burgundy?
Verdiccio di Matelica or Greco di Tufo

Red Burgundy?
Barolo or Barbaresco or Etna Rosso

Champagne?
Franciacorta or Trento

Californian Zinfandel?
Primitivo di Manduria

Torrontes?
Moscato Fiori d'Arancio Colli Euganei

Chablis?
Soave

Cote de Provenece Rosè?
Bardolino Chiaretto or Cerasuolo d'Abruzzo

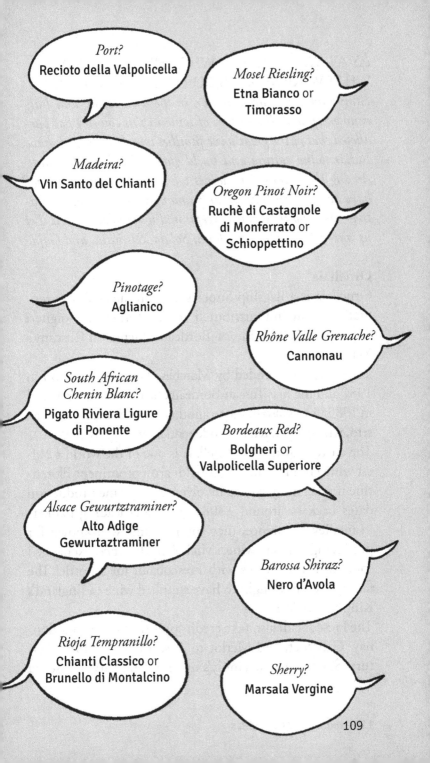

AY AY AY! - WHO ARE WHO THE "AIAS" AND WHAT WINE STORIES DO THEY HAVE TO TELL?

Family businesses are common in the wine sector, and Italy is no exception. The history of wine in this country has paralleled that of the great wine families who have helped shape Italian wine culture and build globally recognised brands. Among the brands, four wines whose names end with "aia" have been regarded as not only amongst the finest representatives, but also those with exceptional wine stories to tell. Let us introduce you to: Ornellaia, Solaia, Sassicaia, and Gaja.

Ornellaia

Ornellaia is a flagship Supertuscan producer whose reputation is mainly attributed to the Ornellaia Bolgheri Superiore DOC wine, a Bordeaux blend on Tuscany's Maremma coast.

The estate was founded by Marchese Lodovico Antinori in 1981 and the first Tuscan Bordeaux blend was later released in 1985. It was also home to another Super Tuscan star, Masseto, which separated as a independent winery in 2019.

The current owner of Ornellaia is one of the world's oldest wine families, the Frescobaldi are a prominent Florentine noble family whose involvement in wine production dates back to around 1308. Originally leading bankers in medieval Florence, they soon became well-known for producing Tuscan wine. Michelangelo once exchanged some of his paintings with Frescobaldi for a bottle! The family is even thought to have supplied wine to England's King Henry VIII.

The Frescobladi also take credit for introducing Chardonnay, Cabernet, and Merlot to Tuscany in the 19th Century. Sticking to the family's mission Cultivating Toscana

Diversity, the family fast expanded in the second half 20th century. Now, 10 out of 11 wineries owned by the family are located in Tuscany, including Ornellaia which the family acquired full state in 2005.

Solaia

Solaia is the name of the wine and the vineryard, quite self-explantory, it refers to "a sunny place", indicating the location of the vineyard. Emerging as an experiment to make the best of the remaining Cabernet grapes from making Tignalleno wine, few had anticipated that Solaia would rise us so swiftly to be one of the twin wine stars of Antinori Family.

Originally, Solaia was a blend dirven by Cabernet Sauvignon and Cabernet Franc, and it was not until the substitution of Sangiovese to Cabernet Franc that Solaia took the shape of today. Its twin Tignanello wine is a Sangiovese dominated wine with addition of Cabernet Sauvignon. The Antinori family has been committed to winemaking since 1385 when Giovanni di Piero Antinori became a member, of the "Arte Fiorentina dei Vinattieri", the Florentine Winemakers' Guild.

It is now Italy's biggest family-owned wine group and manages 15 wineries across 5 regions of Italy. Steadily investing abroad, the Antinori family also manages or is partially involved in wine projects in the US, Malta, Hungary, Romania and Chile. Among them, sits the world-famous Stag's Leap, the cult wine from Napa Valley.

Gaja

Gaja is a leading Piedmont producer and is credited for making a wide range of Nebbiolo based wines including the flagship Gaja Barbaresco DOCG wine which dates back to the very beginning of its founding.

Originally came from Spain in the 17th century, the family didn't actually practice winemaking until 1859 when Giovanni Gaja started the adventure with only two hectares of vineyard in Barbaresco. With time, the family gradually improved the wine quality and sized up. By the time the fifth generation, Angelo Gaja, took over the family business, Gaja was already the leading Barbaresco producer with 40 hectares of vineyard, though Barbaresco enjoyed only regional reputation.

Angelo, a trained Enologist with international experience, introduced numerous advanced techniques in both the vineyard and the cellar, initiating the winery's modern success and eventually leading "Barbaresco Gaja", an eponymous wine, to a sought-after iconic wine from Italy. Now the family's winemaking journey has broadened to include Brunello and Bolgheri in Tuscany, and even as far as the Etna region where a joint venue called IDDA was found in collaboration with Etna producer Graci.

Sassicaia

The Incisa della Rocchetta family has its origin in Piedmont, however it was the romantic binding between Mario Incisa Della Rocchetta and Clarice Della Gherardesca that brought winemaking into reality in Bolgheri region of Tuscany where Clarice Della Gherardesca inherited a large piece of land as the dowry to her marriage in 1930.

Mario had long developed an interest in wine and appreciated the Cabernet grapes since his days in Pisa as an enology student. It was no wonder that he later created Tenuta San Guido (named after Saint Guido della Gherardesca who lived during the XI century) and introduced experimental cuttings of Cabernet from his friend's vineyard near Pisa. The first vineyard slot was chosen right next to Castiglioncello in Bolgheri and the soil is so pebbly that it was named as "Sassicaia", meaning the place with many stones.

Whilst initially Mario kept the Sassicaia wines for family consumption only, he was eventually convinced by his son (Nicolò Incisa Della Rocchetta) and his nephew (Piero Antinori) to release the 1968 vintage to the market in 1971. The rest is history.

Lesser known to the wine connoisseurs, the family also has a deep passion for thoroughbred horses and natural life protection. Compared with the area under vine, the Razza Dormello-Olgiata thoroughbred stud farm and the Bird Sanctuary "Padule di Bolgheri" occupy many more lands at Tenuta San Guido.

DRINK AND DRESS TO IMPRESS

If there are two things the Italians (arguably) know how to do better than anyone else in the world, it's dress well and drink well. However, what many people don't realise is that these two things are often inextricably linked. In this chapter we thought it would be fun to show those Italian wineries that are owned by fashion moguls. Afterall If you dress to impress you might as well accessorise the ensemble with a suitably paired glass of wine!

The Ferragamo Family.
Il Borro and Castiglion del Bosco.

Having made the family name thanks to their hand-made leather shoes, the Ferragamo brothers set out to try their hand ("feet"?) at wine. In 1993 Ferruccio Ferragamo bought Il Borro, an idyllic estate nestled in the heart of Tuscany. For more than a decade the family worked on restoring the land and the villa to its original pre-World War II glory and in 2007 the winery finally opened. Today it produces six different wines from not only the classic French varieties of Merlot, Petit Verdot, Cabernet Sauvignon, and Chardonnay, but also Sangiovese. However, what many might find surprising is that their flagship wine, Alessandro Dal Borro is actually 100% Syrah.

Not content with success thanks to shoes and now Syrah, Massimo Ferragamo, Ferruccio's brother and CEO of the family operations in the USA, also succumbed to the desire to pursue wine. Following his brother's footsteps, he purchased an 800-year-old, 4,3000 acre estate in 2003. Also in Tuscany Castiglion de Bosco, is not only one of the region's largest estates, it is also one of the star players, producing critically acclaimed Brunello di Montalcino DOCG wines.

Roberto Cavalli - Tenuta degli Dei

World famous stylist Roberto Cavalli and his son Tommaso take their wines as seriously as they take their fashion, which is why when they planted their Tenuta degli Dei estate in the heart of the Chianti Classico region of Tuscany they enlisted the help of renowned enologist Carlo Ferrini. Despite being in this famous DOCG region it is actually for the IGT blends of Merlot, Cabernet Sauvignon, Cabernet Franc, Petit Verdot and Alicante Bouschet that the estate is best known. Whilst Tommaso never truly wanted to follow his father into fashion the wines haven't quite managed to escape the stylistic touch of a fashionista, with a special Cavalli Selection, which, for each vintage, includes a different Roberto Cavalli design. Indeed, the choice for the debut 2004 got the full Roberto touch with a leopard-skin texture! But don't worry, Tommaso and Ferrini are continuing to strive to make sure these wines are recognisable by their quality not their quirky packaging.

Renzo Rosso - Diesel Farm

Situated in the hills of Marostica in the Veneto is the somewhat intriguingly named "Diesel Farm". The winery name becomes more intuitive when you realise that it is the brainchild of Renzo Russo, founder of the Diesel fashion house. He owns 100 hectares of south-facing vineyards occupied with Merlot, Cabernet Sauvignon, Chardonnay and Pinot Nero. These last two are particularly interesting because his limestone soils give him the perfect opportunity for the production of his sparkling wine, which is elegantly named "Bolle di Rosso". All the wines are presented in simple black bottles that mirror the slightly industrial style of the fashion brand, and yet the wines themselves are anything but industrial, with Russo and his team adhere to strict organic principles and artisanal production methods.

Famiglia Marzotto - Santa Margherita

There has long been an historical connection between wool and wine, with the Venetians using wine as a trading tool in order to secure wool and dyes. Perhaps textile magnates Marzotto were aware of this when they flexed their industrious muscles and expanded into agriculture? In 1935 Gaetano Marzotto purchased a thousand hectares of perfect land in the Veneto and soon begin producing not only wines, but other products under a brand name chosen to immortalise his beloved companion, Margherita Lampertico Marzotto. Thus, Santa Margherita was born. Now the estate produces everything from sparkling to red wines and is working hard to becoming a carbon neutral operation.

Moretti Polegato - Villa Sandi

For some, it is the wine that comes first, not the fashion. Mario Moretti Polegato – who in modern Italian business may be best known for his stewardship of the Geox shoe empire – actually studied oenology and was born into a family already connect with a deep winemaking history. In fact, it was whilst at a wine trade fair that he had the idea that would revolutionise footwear and catapult him into another world entirely. However, he has always maintained his passion for food and wine, as is demonstrated by the success of Villa Sandi, his wine estate known primarily for its exceptional sparkling wines from Cartizze.

Giovanni Bulgari - Podernuovo a Palazzone

Let's not forget that an outfit isn't complete without accessories and therefore it would be rude not to include famous jeweler Giovanni Bulgari and his estate Podernuovo a Palazzone. Again, we see Tuscany returning as a common theme, and Sangiovese as a key protagonist with Bulgari wanting to maintain the tradition of the area. But of course, he could not resist the pull of the international grapes that have proven to perform so well in the area and thus his other two wines put Cabernet Franc and then Cabernet Sauvignon, Merlot and surprise addition Montepulciano to the fore. Given the attention to detail and precious stones (themselves a product of nature) that his background in jewelry making bring him, it will be of no surprise to hear that Bulgari's main aim with these wines was to demonstrate elegance, humility and a respect for the environment, throw in that he grew up just a stone's throw away in his family home in Cordoba and you cannot help but feel his passion for this project.

And of course, it's not just brands producing wine.... Dolce&Gabbana recently launched their new collection with an advert shot in the vineyard of the Canneto winery in Montepulciano. It seems that vines will never go out of style...

BASIC WINE DICTIONARY

Abboccato: off-dry
Acidità: acidity
Amabile: semisweet; demisec
Amaro: bitter
Annata: vintage
Appassimento: the process of drying grapes
Aromatico: aromatic; having a rich, usually floral, aroma
Assemblaggio: blending
Bianco: white
Bicchiere: wineglass; drinking glass
Biodinamica: biodynamic
Biologica: organic
Bollicine: bubbles
Botte: wine barrel
Bottiglia: bottle
Cantina: cellar; winery
Cavatappi: corkscrew
Classico: classic, often used in reference to a historic wine region or a traditional style)
Consorzio: consortium, especially of wine producers in a specific region
Denominazione: denomination; appellation; place-name
Dolce: sweet
Dosaggio: dosage
Enoteca: wine shop; wine bar
Equilibrato: balanced
Etichetta: label
Fresco: fresh
Frizzante: effervescent; fizzy; sparkling *(spumante)*

Liquoroso: fortified; with added alcohol

Millesimato: vintage dated, usually referring to sparkling wine

Passito: wine made using partially dried grapes to increase the alcohol and/or sweetness level

Qualità: quality

Rosato: pink or rosé wine

Rosso: red

Secco: dry

Spumante: sparkling (wine)

Tannico: tannic

Tappo: closure

Uva: grape

Uvaggio: blend of grapes

Varietà: variety

Vendemmia: harvest

Vendemmia tardiva: late harvest

Vigna: vineyard (pl. *vigne*)

Vino: wine

Vitigno: grape variety (pl. *vitigni*)

barrique   tonneau   botte

ITALIAN WINE TERMS PRONUNCIATIONS

Italian Wine Regions

- **Abruzzo** (ah-BROOT-zo)
- **Aosta Valley** (Ah-OH-stah)
  *Italian: **Valle D'Aosta** (VAHL-leh; DOH-stah)*
- **Apulia** (ah-POOL-yah)
  *Italian: **Puglia** (POOL-yah)*
- **Basilicata** (bah-zee-lee-KAH-tah)
- **Calabria** (cah-LAH-bree-ah)
- **Campania** (cahm-PAH-nee-ah)
- **Emilia Romagna** (eh-MEE-lee-ah; ro-MAH-n'yah)
- **Friuli-Venezia Giulia** (FREE-oo-lee; veh-NET-zee-ah; JOO-lee-ah)
- **Lazio** (LAH-t'zee-oh)
- **Liguria** (lee-GOO-ree-yah)
- **Lombardy** (LOM-bar-dee)
  *Italian: **Lombardia** (lom-bar-DEE-ah)*
- **Marche** (MAR-keh)
- **Molise** (moh-LEE-zeh)
- **Piedmont** (PEED-mont)
  *Italian: **Piemonte** (pee-MON-teh)*
- **Sardinia** (sar-DIN-EE-ah)
  *Italian: **Sardegna** (sar-DEHN-ya)*
- **Sicily** (SI-sil-ee)
  *Italian: **Sicilia** (see-CHEEL-yah)*
- **Trentino-Alto Adige** (tren-TEE-noh; AL-toh; AH-dee-jay)
- **Tuscany** (TUSK-an-ee)
  *Italian: **Toscana** (toss-KAH-nah)*
- **Umbria** (OOM-bree-ah)
- **Veneto** (VEH-neh-toh)

Some Italian Grape Varieties

Aglianico (ahl-YAN-ee-coh)
Arneis (ar-Nae-ees)
Barbera (bar-BEH-rah)
Cannonau (cahn-noh-NOW)
Catarratto (kah-tahr-RAHT-toh)
Cesanese (cheh-sah-NEH-zeh)
Dolcetto (dohl-CHET-toh)
Erbaluce (air-bah-LOO-cheh)
Falanghina (fah-lahn-GHEE-nah)
Fiano (fee-AH-noh)
Gaglioppo (gah-L'YEE'OHP-poh)
Garganega (gahr-GAH-neh-gah)
Glera (GLEH-rah)
Greco (GREH-co)
Grechetto (greh-KEHT-toh)
Lagrein (lah-GRAH'EEN)
Lambrusco (lahm-BROO-sko)
Malvasia (mahl-vah-ZEE-ah)
Montepulciano (MOHN-teh-pool-CHEE'AH-noh)
Nebbiolo (nehb-bee'OH-loh)
Negroamaro (NEH-groh-ah-MAH-roh)
Nero d'Avola (NEH-roh;-DAH-voh-lah)
Nerello Mascalese (neh-REHL-loh; MAHS-kah-LEH-zeh)
Pigato (pee-GAH-toh)
Pinot Bianco (PEE-noh; B'YAHN-coh)
Pinot Grigio (PEE-noh; GREE-joe)
Pinot Nero (PEE-noh; NEH-roh)
Primitivo (pree-mee-TEE-voh)

Sagrantino (SAH-grahn-TEE-noh)
Sangiovese (SAHN-joh-VEH-zeh)
Schioppettino (skee'ohp-peht-TEE-noh)
Teroldego (the-ROHL-deh-goh)
Trebbiano (treb-bee-AH-noh)
Verdicchio (vehr-DEEK-key-oh)
Verduzzo (vehr-DOO-tsoh)
Vermentino (vehr-mehn-TEE-noh)

Sneak Peek to Italian Wine Market

Italy a country where the diverse terrains meet creative vintners, all 20 regions of the country grow wine grapes thanks to the countless combination of climate, soil conditions, and native grapes.

Not only Italy is one of the world's oldest wine-producing countries, but it has also remained the world's largest wine producer since it overtook France in 2015, though the vineyard surface of Italy ranks only the 4th, after Spain, China, and France.

With an area of 705,000 hectares under vineyard cultivation, Italy produced 46.6 million hl of wine in 2019, accounting for 18% of global production. Whereas all 20 regions of Italy are practicing vine growing and winemaking, a gap in production capacity exists.

SPAIN	CHINA	FRANCE	ITALY	TURKEY
VINEYARD SURFACE	VINEYARD SURFACE	VINEYARD SURFACE	VINEYARD SURFACE	VINEYARD SURFACE
969	**875**	**793**	**705**	**448**
(x 1000 ha)	(x 1000 ha)	(x 1000 ha)	(x 1000 ha)	(x 1000 ha)

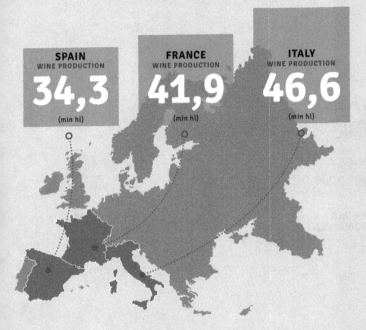

SPAIN WINE PRODUCTION	FRANCE WINE PRODUCTION	ITALY WINE PRODUCTION
34,3 (mln hl)	**41,9** (mln hl)	**46,6** (mln hl)

The mountainous Valle d'Aosta, costal Liguria and southern Basilicata and Molise represent the lower end of the spectrum, while Veneto, Puglia and Emilia Romagna are the three highest producing regions, taking up over 50% of the national wine production. Italy is a notable white wine-producing country, led by Veneto, Friuli-Venezia Giulia, Lazio, and Trentino-Alto Adige, white wine accounted for 57% of Italy's wine production in 2018.

Focusing on quality wine production, Italy has significantly increased the percentage of wine production in the DOP (DOC or DOCG) category over the past 2 decades. On average, more than 40% of the wines made in Italy are PDO wines and this is 10% more compared to that of 2010.

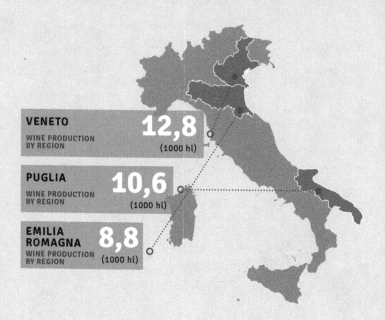

VENETO
WINE PRODUCTION BY REGION
12,8
(1000 hl)

PUGLIA
WINE PRODUCTION BY REGION
10,6
(1000 hl)

EMILIA ROMAGNA
WINE PRODUCTION BY REGION
8,8
(1000 hl)

Wine culture is popular domestically among Italians, who consume an average of 44 liters per capita, ranking third in world wine consumption. Most Italians develop a special connection with the wines produced in their home area and 19% of them consume Italian wine daily, enjoying more than 22 million hl of wines. However, there is still an enough production to guarantee Italy a huge platform in the international market.

Italian wine is incredibly popular among wine lovers in all corners of the globe. As a major wine exporter in the world, Italy ranks second in both volume and value. Its main export destinations include Germany, the US, the UK, Switzerland, and Canada.

Meanwhile, new emerging wine consumption countries such as Russia and China are gradually catching up and

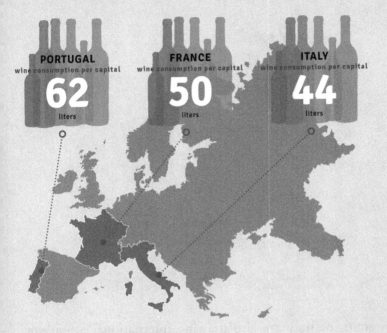

PORTUGAL
wine consumption per capital
62
liters

FRANCE
wine consumption per capital
50
liters

ITALY
wine consumption per capital
44
liters

starting to develop a taste for Italian wine. Among the many categories of Italian wine, Sparkling wine has seen major growth with 20% of Italian export in terms of volume consisting of sparkling wines.

The 408 PDOs wines are spreading across the 20 different regions, but most of them are concentrated in Piedmont, Lombardy, the Veneto, and Tuscany. Among these are appellations appreciated and sought after by wine lovers around the world: Amarone Della Valpolicella, Barolo, Barbaresco, Brunello di Montalcino, Chianti and the Supertuscans (known as the "ABBBCS").

Other notable wines that have gained attention in recent years in the international markets and among specialists are a trio of sparkling wines; Prosecco, Trento DOC and Franciacorta. Quality native grapes from the centre and

USA
ITALY'S MAJOR
EXPORT DESTINATION
1431
(euro milions)

GERMANY
ITALY'S MAJOR
EXPORT DESTINATION
1021
(euro milions)

UNITED
KINGDOM
ITALY'S MAJOR
EXPORT DESTINATION
808
(euro milions)

south of Italy are also drawing international attention: Aglianico, Verdicchio, Sagrantino, Nero d'Avola and Nerello Mascalese among others.

Italy hold some impressive figures: 1 country, 20 regions, 408 DOP wines, 570 officially registered varieties, 705 thousand hectares of vineyards, over 300 thousand wine-growers, over 40 million hl wine produced every year. It is a country riding a wave of renewed interest, with the world's wine lovers welcoming its wines into the marketplace. It's now the time for Italian wine producers to showcase their individual talents and share the story of the countless native wine grapes.

LEARN MORE ABOUT ITALIAN WINES

If this book has enlightened and encouraged you to speak confidently about Italian wines with your friends and family, you may also consider looking for more other available resources, here are some that we highly recommend!

ITALIAN WINE BOOKS
(Find out more at www.italianwinebook.com)

Italian Wine Unplugged *by Stevie Kim (General Editor) and contributors: Geralyn Brostrom, Lingzi He, Michaela Morris, Michele Longo, and JC Viens.*
A comprehensive cultural and scientific introduction to Italian wines and its hundreds of native grapes - This information is organised in accessible, color-coded and easy-to-read entries. www.italianwineunplugged.com.

Sangiovese, Lambrusco, and Other Vine Stories
by Professor Attilio Scienza and Serena Imazio
These writings explore the cultivation of grape vines, along with the history of human communities that influenced the production and trading of Italian wines. It follows the lineage of wine through discussion of origin and ancestry of vines such as Sangiovese, Ribolla, Primitivo and the many Moscato, Malvasia, and Lambrusco grapes.

#nofilter: 12 Q&A with Italian Wine Influencers
by Stevie Kim
This book gives a snapshot of wine influencer scene in Italy. This is a collection of interviews with 9 Italian wine influencers who openly discuss their work and love for

wine. They provide tips on becoming an influencer and share advice on how wineries can harness the potential of social media.

ITALIAN WINE PODCAST

A podcast dedicated to the Italian Wine World. Monty Waldin uncovers the unique Italian winemaking tradition in conversation with some of its key protagonists. This podcast aims to inform, educate, and entertain listeners about Italian wine through engaging conversations with producers, experts and personalities of the Italian wine scene. It also features mini-masterclasses on grape varieties thanks to dedicated interviews with Prof. Attilio Scienza available for free on Soundcloud, iTunes, Ximalaya and Spotify. (italianwinepodcast.com)

VINITALY INTERNATIONAL ACADEMY

Vinitaly International Academy (VIA) aims to be the gold standard of Italian wine education. VIA offers a complete educational path with standardised courses that will teach professionals and educators to master the diversity of Italian wine in a rigorous, organized manner. Find out more at www.vinitalyinternational.com/vinitaly-international-academy

BIBLIOGRAPHY
The following sources are re-adapted by the authors

From Bacchus to Cavour

Leonardo Da Vinci

WEBFOODCULTURE. *Leonardo da Vinci and wine*. n.d. 2020. <www.webfoodculture.com/leonardo-da-vinci-wine/>.

O'DONELL, B., MUSTACICH, S., FISH, T. *Renaissance man's wine reborn: inside Leonardo da Vinci's vineyard.* 9 July 2019. <www.winespectator.com/articles/renaissance-man-s-wine-reborn-inside-leonardo-da-vinci-s-milan-vineyard-unfiltered>.

Medici

CERNILLI, D. *Cosimo III and his descendants*. 10 October 2016. <www.doctorwine.it/en/signed-doctorwine/signed-dw/cosimo-iii-and-his-descendants>.

Cavour

CONTI, S. *La storia del Baroloe del conte di Cavour*. 22 October 2019. <www.lastampa.it/torino/2011/01/02/news/la-storia-del-baroloe-del-conte-di-cavour-1.36981594>.

CABUTTO, L. *The winegrowing count of Cavour*. n.d. Az. Agricola Le Ginestre. <www.leginestre.com/en/historic-wine-cellar-langhe/the-winegrowing-count-of-cavour/>.

Top 10 Grape List

VITISPHERE. *13 grape varieties cover one third of global vineyard acreage*. 4 January 2018. <www.vitisphere.com/news-86722-13-grape-varieties-cover-one-third-of-global-vineyard-acreage.htm>.

BACCAGLIO, M. *I principali vitigni del mondo e per nazione: aggiornamento OIV 2017*. 8 April 2018. <www.inumeridelvino.it/2018/04/i-principali-vitigni-del-mondo-e-per-nazione-aggiornamento-oiv-2017.html#comments>.

OIV - ORGANISATION INTERNATIONALE DE LA VIGNE ET DU VIN. *Distribution of the world's grapevine varieties.* Focus report. Paris, 2017. <www.oiv.int/public/medias/5888/en-distribution-of-the-worlds-grapevine-varieties.pdf>.

Top 5 Pdos

ITALIAN WINE CENTRAL. *Prosecco DOC.* n.d. Vindeavour. 2020. <italianwinecentral.com/denomination/prosecco-doc/>.

SINIGALIA, A. *Pinot Grigio delle Venezie: nasce la DOC.* February 2017. Associazione Italiana Sommelier Veneto. <www.aisveneto.it/news/465-pinot-grigio-delle-venezie-nasce-la-doc.html#.XpWVkVP7TMJ>.

SCHIESSL, C. *The definitive guide to the regions of Chianti (with map).* 6 August 2017. VinePair. <vinepair.com/articles/definitive-guide-regions-chianti-map/>.

ASSOCIAZIONE NAZIONALE PRODUTTORI VINICOLI E TURISMO DEL VINO. *ASTI DOCG.* 31 October 2020. <www.assovini.it/italia/piemonte/item/319-asti-docgDe>.

DE CRISTOFARO, P. *50 years of Montepulciano d'Abruzzo, a territorial discovery.* 12 March 2018. Gambero Rosso SPA. <www.gamberorosso.it/en/uncategorized-en/50-years-of-montepulciano-d-abruzzo-a-territorial-discovery/>.

Ay ay ay! - Who are who the "aias" and what wine stories do they have to tell?

FORBES ITALIA. *Le 100 famiglie imprenditoriali italiane.* 10 March 2018. <forbes.it/classifica/100-famiglie-imprenditoriali-italiane-forbes/>.

MEDIOBANCA - BANCA DI CREDITO FINANZIARIO
SPA. *Wine industry survey*. Milan: Mediobanca- Area Studi, 2019.
<www.mbres.it/sites/default/files/resources/download_en/Wine_
Survey_2019.pdf>.

Solaia

FRANK, M. *Top 100 of 2016: the family trust*. 30 April 2016. Wine
Spectator Online. <top100.winespectator.com/article/the-family-
trust/>.

GALLONI, A. *Antinori Solaia - a complete retrospective 1978-2010*.
2020. <vinous.com/articles/antinori-solaia-a-complete-retrospective-
1978-2010-dec-2013>.

ITALIAN WINE MERCHANTS. *Antinori*. n.d. <www.
italianwinemerchants.com/Antinori-s/161.htm>.

Ornellaia

MEININGER. *Marchesi de' Frescobaldi - 30 generations of Tuscany*.
28 October 2013. <www.wine-business-international.com/wine/
families-wine-sponsored-

LAWRENCE, J. *10 things every wine lover should know about
Ornellaia*. 5 January 2016. <www.wine-searcher.com/m/2016/01/10-
things-every-wine-lover-should-know-about-ornellaia>.

Gaja

CERNILLI, D. *Sono usciti i vini di Idda, l'azienda etnera di Gaja e
Graci*. 28 February 2020. <www.doctorwine.it/degustazioni/note-
di-degustazione/sono-usciti-i-vini-di-idda-l-azienda-etnea-di-gaja-e-
graci>.

TERLATO WINES. *Gaja: History*. n.d. 2020. <www.terlatowines.
com/brands/italy/gaja/history>.

ATKINS, T. *10 things every wine lover should know about Gaja*. 2
October 2014. <www.wine-searcher.com/m/2014/10/10-things-
every-wine-lover-should-know-about-gaja>.

Sassicaia

TENUTA SAN GUIDO. n.d. 2020. <www.tenutasanguido.com/
eng/index.html>.

O'KEEFE, K. *Italy's sassy wine superstar*. 13 December 2012. <www.
wine-searcher.com/m/2012/12/sassicaia-sassy-seductive-superstar-of-
italian-wine>.

MCKIRDY, T. *7 things you should know about Ornellaia*. 20
September 2019. <vinepair.com/articles/ornellaia-tuscany-guide/>.

NICKLIN, H. *The story of Sassicaia: Italy's first Super Tuscan*. 20
September 2018. <www.winerist.com/magazine/ask-winerist/the-
story-of-sassicaia-italys-first-super-tuscan>.

Sneak Peek to Italian Wine Market

OIV - ORGANISATION INTERNATIONALE DE LA VIGNE
ET DU VIN. *Distribution of the world's grapevine varieties*.
Focus report. Paris, 2017. <www.oiv.int/public/medias/5888/en-
distribution-of-the-worlds-grapevine-varieties.pdf>.

Italian Wine Terms & Pronunciations

ITALIAN WINE CENTRAL. *Glossary of Italian wine terms*. n.d.
Vindeavour. <italianwinecentral.com/glossary-alphabetical/>.

ITALIAN TRADE AGENCY (ICE) ITALIAN TRADE
COMMISSION. *Italian wine terms & pronunciation guide*. 2020.
<extraordinaryitalianwine.us/learn/italian-wine-terms-pronunciation-
guide/>.

MARCIS, R. *Italian wine terms*. 6 July 2017. <www.
winewordswisdom.com/aboutitalwine/italian_wine_terms.html>.

Other References

SCIENZA, A., M. WALDIN and et al. "Italian Wine Podcast." Verona, 2017. Podcast.

FANCIULLI, J. *Personal communications* March 2020.

POSITIVE PRESS SAS. 2017. <italianwinebook.com/>.

RAYE, S. *How to get US market-ready: book to be released Nov. 26.* 31 October 2018. <bevologyinc.com/blog/2018/10/31/get-u-s-market-ready-book-released-nov-26/>.

BROSTROM, G., et al. *Italian Wine Unplugged Grape by Grape.* Ed. S. KIM. Verona: Positive Press, 2017.

ROBINSON, J. *The 24-hour wine expert.* London: Penguin Books, 2016.

LAWRENCE, R. *Personal communications and notes* March 2020.

ABOUT THE AUTHORS

Dr Rebecca Lawrence DipWSET is an educator, editor and consultant specialising in Italian wine. She develops global education courses, leads the Vinitaly International Academy Certified Educator programme, and is an educator for the Wine and Spirits Education Trust.

Jacopo Fanciulli, VIA Italian Wine Ambassador and DipWSET Candidate. He has a degree in Communication Sciences, and Masters degrees in Enology and Marketing. He's a Sommelier and AIS Taster and ans has been a second stage Master of Wine Student.

Lyka Caparas, MBA, WSET Level 3, is a wine writer and product development marketing expert. She is finishing her 2nd Masters in Erasmus Wine Tourism.

Lan LIU, MBA, WSET Level 3, is the coordinator of Vinitaly International Academy and a certified Italian wine ambassador. He obtained his bachelor's degree in Enology in China and furthered his wine passion in France, receiving a Master's Degree in Enology.

Silvia Albano is a graphic designer and illustrator. Silvia's hobbies include sharing her misadventures with her followers through the comic "Le mie malattie".